PUPIL
TEXTBOOK
6B

Noogol

Googol

Koogol

Ooogol

Zoogol

Toogol

Consultant and author
Dr Fong Ho Kheong

Authors
Gan Kee Soon and Chelvi Ramakrishnan

UK consultants
Carole Skinner, Simon d'Angelo and Elizabeth Gibbs

Published by Marshall Cavendish Education
Times Centre, 1 New Industrial Road, Singapore 536196
Customer Service Hotline: (65) 6213 9444
Email: tmesales@mceducation.com
Website: www.mceducation.com

Distributed by
Oxford University Press
Great Clarendon Street, Oxford,
OX2 6DP, United Kingdom
www.oxfordprimary.co.uk
www.oxfordowl.co.uk

First published 2015
Reprinted 2015

ISBN 978-981-01-8906-8

Printed in China

Acknowledgements
Written by Dr Fong Ho Kheong, Gan Kee Soon and Chelvi Ramakrishnan

UK consultants: Carole Skinner, Simon d'Angelo and Elizabeth Gibbs

Cover artwork by Daron Parton

The authors and publisher would like to thank all schools and individuals
who helped to trial and review Inspire Maths resources.

Introduction

Inspire Maths is a comprehensive, activity-based programme designed to provide pupils with a firm foundation in maths and to develop creative and critical thinking skills to become fluent problem solvers.

Inspire Maths makes learning maths fun and rewarding through the use of engaging illustrations and games that help to reinforce and consolidate learning.

For the teacher:

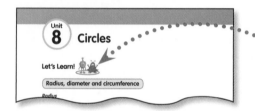

Use the engaging and highly scaffolded **Let's Learn!** to introduce concepts. Integrated questions allow for immediate assessment and consolidation of concepts learnt.

Carry out investigative activities in **Let's Explore!** These allow pupils to apply concepts learnt.

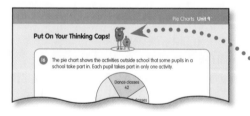

Challenge pupils to solve non-routine questions by applying relevant heuristics and thinking skills in **Put On Your Thinking Caps!**

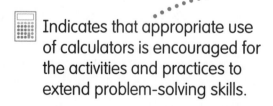 Indicates that appropriate use of calculators is encouraged for the activities and practices to extend problem-solving skills.

For the parent/guardian:

Build home-school links and make maths come alive by using the tips in Home Maths to help children apply mathematical concepts to daily life.

For the pupil:

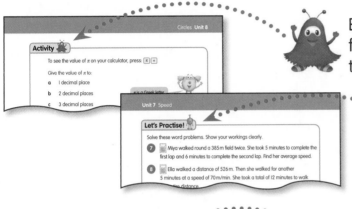

Enjoy **Inspire Maths** with your friends. Explore your learning through activities and group work.

Let's Practise! contains questions that provide opportunities for further practice.

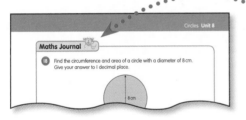

Share what you have learnt, create your own questions and become aware of your own mathematical thinking in your Maths Journal.

Recall skills from earlier years and link them to new concepts in the current unit.

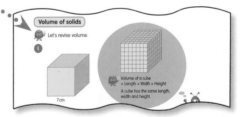

Let's Wrap It Up! summarises the concepts you have learnt in the current unit, while **Let's Revise!** provides a worked example that covers the key concepts for ease of revision.

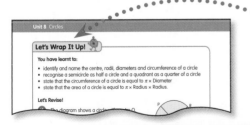

Use the worked examples and questions to help you understand problem-solving strategies.

Contents

Speed

Let's Learn!

Distance and speed

1. Mr Smith is driving from Peterstown to Philipstown. In 1 hour, he drove 65 km. Mr Williams is also driving in the same direction. In 1 hour, he drove 95 km.

Mr Smith is driving at a speed of 65 km per hour.

Mr Williams is driving at a speed of 95 km per hour.

The **speed** tells us how fast Mr Smith and Mr Williams are travelling.

We can write the speed of Mr Smith's car as 65 km/h.
In the same way, we can write the speed of Mr Williams' car as 95 km/h.

The symbol **/** means **per**.
So we read 65 km/h as
65 km per hour.

We express speed
as distance travelled
per unit of time.

Answer these questions.

2 **a**   Jack can cycle 8 km in 1 hour.
His speed is ⬚ km/h.

b   Ella can run 300 m in 1 minute.
Her speed is ⬚ m/min.

c   A marble rolls 9 cm in 1 second.
Its speed is ⬚ cm/s.

d   Tai throws a ball and it falls 2 m in 1 second.
Its speed is ⬚ m/s.

3 **a**   Hardeep runs at a speed of 12·5 m/s.
In 1 s, he runs ⬚ m.

b   A lorry travelled at a speed of 48 km/h.
In 1 h, the lorry travelled ⬚ km.

3

Mr Adams drives his lorry at a speed of 45 km/h. At this speed, how far does Mr Adams travel in:

a 2 hours?

b 5 hours?

45 km/h means 45 km per hour.

In 1 hour, Mr Adams travels 45 km.

In 2 hours, Mr Adams travels 45 × 2 = 90 km.

In 5 hours, Mr Adams travels 45 × 5 = 225 km.

Speed   Time   Distance

$D = S \times T$

Distance = Speed × Time

 Home Maths
Tell your child the time at which you leave work and the time at which you arrive home. Ask your child to calculate how long it takes you to travel from work back to your home.

5 A racing car is travelling at a speed of 175 km/h on a race track. How far can it travel in 3 hours?

Method I

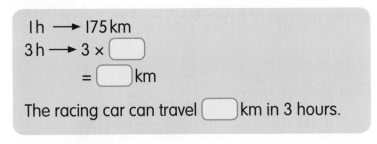

1 h ⟶ 175 km
3 h ⟶ 3 × ▢
= ▢ km

The racing car can travel ▢ km in 3 hours.

Speed = ▢ km/h

Method 2

Speed = ▢ km/h
Time = ▢ h
Distance = Speed × Time
= ▢ × ▢
= ▢ km

The racing car can travel ▢ km in 3 hours.

6 An aeroplane can travel at a speed of 250 m/s. How far can the plane travel in 2 seconds?

Method I

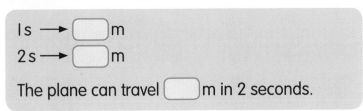

1 s ⟶ ▢ m
2 s ⟶ ▢ m

The plane can travel ▢ m in 2 seconds.

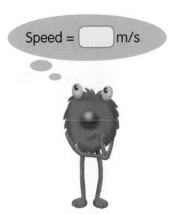

Speed = ▢ m/s

Method 2

Speed = ▢ m/s
Time = ▢ s
Distance = ▢ × ▢
= ▢ m

The plane can travel ▢ m in 2 seconds.

Speed involves two quantities:

a   Distance covered

b   Time taken.

Speed is the distance covered per unit of time.

Example

A snail crawls at a speed of 20 cm/min.

20 cm   ——————▶   I minute
(distance covered)   (per unit time)

The snail covers 20 cm per minute.

---

7   Millie swims 450 m in 10 minutes. Find her swimming speed in m/min.

Method I

10 mins ⟶ 450 m

I min   ⟶ $\dfrac{450}{10}$

              = 45 m

Millie's swimming speed is 45 m/min.

> To find the speed in m/min means to find the distance she swims in I minute.

Method 2

Distance = 450 m
Time = 10 mins

Speed = Distance ÷ Time

Speed = 450 ÷ 10
       = 45 m/min

Millie's swimming speed is 45 m/min.

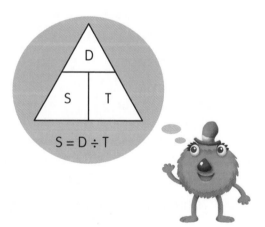

$S = D \div T$

Home Maths
Help your child to calculate their average speed for swimming 2 lengths of a pool. Use a stopwatch to find the time taken for their swim.

8 The distance between Smithstown and Jamestown is 147 km. A van takes 3 hours to travel from Smithstown to Jamestown. What is the speed of the van?

Method 1

3 h ⟶ ☐ km
1 h ⟶ ☐ ÷ 3
    = ☐ km

The speed of the van is ☐ km/h.

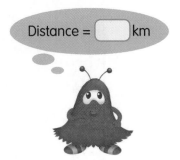

Distance = ☐ km

Method 2

Distance = ☐ km
Time = ☐ h
Speed = Distance ÷ Time
    = ☐ km/h

The speed of the van is ☐ km/h.

9 An athlete ran round a field at a speed of 8 m/s. How long did he take to run a distance of 96 m?

Method 1

8 m ⟶ 1 s
96 m ⟶ $\frac{96}{8}$
    = 12 s

The athlete took 12 s to run 96 m.

Method 2

Distance = 96 m
Speed = 8 m/s

Time = Distance ÷ Speed

Time = 96 ÷ 8
    = 12 s

The athlete took 12 s to run 96 m.

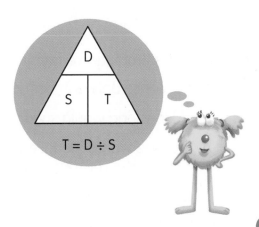

$T = D \div S$

10 The distance between Stonebury and Middlewater is 216 km. Mr Thomas rides his moped at a speed of 54 km/h. How long will Mr Thomas take to travel from Stonebury to Middlewater?

Method 1

☐ km ⟶ 1 h
☐ km ⟶ ☐ h

Mr Thomas will take ☐ h to travel from Stonebury to Middlewater.

Method 2

Distance = ☐ km
Speed = ☐ km/h
Time = Distance ÷ Speed
     = ☐ h

Mr Thomas will take ☐ h to travel from Stonebury to Middlewater.

Speed = ☐ km/h

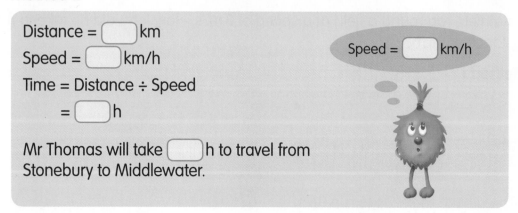

11 Miss Brook drove from her house to the supermarket at a speed of 18 m/s. The distance between her house and the supermarket was 1008 m.

a How long would she take to drive from her house to the supermarket?

b If she wanted to take 14 s less to get to the supermarket, at what speed must she drive?

a   Time = Distance ÷ Speed

   = ⬚ ÷ ⬚

   = ⬚ s

Miss Brook took ⬚ s to drive from her house to the supermarket.

b   Time = ⬚ – 14

   = ⬚ s

Speed = Distance ÷ Time

   = ⬚ ÷ ⬚

   = ⬚ m/s

Miss Brook must drive at a speed of ⬚ m/s if she wanted to take 14 s less to get to the supermarket.

Let's Explore!

12   Work in groups of four.

Your teacher will give you a stopwatch and some round objects of different sizes.

1   On the floor, mark out two points, X and Y. The two points should be 100 cm apart.

X ——————————————————————— Y
                      100 cm

2   Roll each object from X to Y. Use the stopwatch to find the time taken for each object to roll from X to Y. Draw a table like the one on the next page and record the time to the nearest second.

Let's Explore!

3 Calculate the speed of each object. What do you observe about the speed of the object and size of the object?

Example

Object	Distance (cm)	Time Taken (s)	Speed (cm/s) (Distance ÷ Time)
A	100		
B	100		
C	100		
D	100		
E	100		

4 Which object rolled the fastest and which object rolled the slowest?

5 Explain the meaning of speed to your partner.

Let's Practise!

Solve these word problems. Show your workings clearly.

13 A driver takes 80 minutes to travel 120 km. Find his speed.

14 Ruby accidentally lets go of the balloon she is holding. It rises 42 m in 8 seconds. What is the speed at which the balloon rises?

15 A skydiver falls at a speed of 3200 m/min. What is the distance the skydiver falls in 4 minutes?

16 A bat can fly at a speed of 48 km/h. How many minutes will it take to fly a distance of 8 km?

Let's Practise!

17 Peter walks from school to his house at a speed of 5 km/h. He takes 20 minutes to get home. What is the distance between school and his house? Give your answer to 2 decimal places.
(Hint: Convert the time from minutes to hours.)

18 A car travelled at a speed of 54 km/h for $3\frac{1}{4}$ h. Find the distance travelled.

19 The distance between Berrytown and Smithsville is 45 km.

a If a car travels at a speed of 60 km/h, how long will it take to travel from Berrytown to Smithsville?

b If the car takes 40 mins to travel from Berrytown to Smithsville, what is the speed of the car? Give your answer in km/min.
Give your answer to 1 decimal place.

Practice Book 6B, p.1

Let's Learn!

Average speed

1 Point A and Point B are 120 m apart. Point B and Point C are 300 m apart. Daniel runs from Point A to Point B in 15 seconds. Then he runs from Point B to Point C in 55 seconds. Find Daniel's average speed for the distance from Point A to Point C.

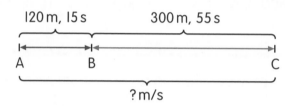

Speed between Point A and Point B is different from speed between Point B and Point C.

Average speed is the average distance travelled per unit of time.

$$\text{Average speed} = \frac{\text{Total distance travelled}}{\text{Total time taken}}$$

Total distance from Point A to Point C = 120 + 300
= 420 m

Total time taken to run from Point A to Point C = 15 + 55
= 70 s

Average speed = $\dfrac{\text{Total distance travelled}}{\text{Total time taken}}$

= $\dfrac{420}{70}$

= 6 m/s

Daniel's average speed is 6 m/s.

2 Mr Clark takes 2 hours to drive from Peterstown to Pinesville. He takes another 3 hours to drive from Pinesville to Smithstown. The distance between Peterstown and Pinesville is 90 km while the distance between Pinesville and Smithstown is 180 km. What is Mr Clark's average speed for the whole journey?

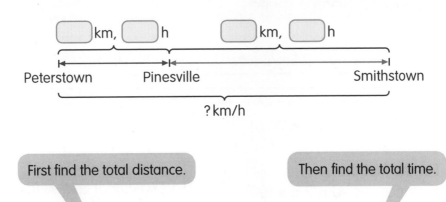

First find the total distance.

Then find the total time.

Total distance from Peterstown to Smithstown = ⬜ + ⬜

= ⬜ km

Total time to travel from Peterstown to Smithstown = ⬜ + ⬜

= ⬜ h

Average speed = $\dfrac{\text{Total distance travelled}}{\text{Total time taken}}$

$= \dfrac{\boxed{}}{\boxed{}}$

= ⬜ km/h

Average speed
$= \dfrac{\text{Total distance travelled}}{\text{Total time taken}}$

Mr Clark's average speed for the whole journey is ⬜ km/h.

3 Millie cycled for 100 seconds at a speed of 2·5 m/s. Then she cycled for another 150 m. In total, she took 200 seconds to complete the bike ride.

a Find the total distance Millie cycled.

b Find Millie's average speed.

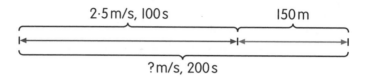

a For the first part,
Distance cycled = 2·5 × 100
= 250 m

Total distance cycled = 250 + 150
= 400 m

Distance = Speed × Time

b Average speed = $\frac{400}{200}$
= 2 m/s

Millie's average speed was 2 m/s.

4 Mr Patel drove for $2\frac{1}{5}$ h at a speed of 70 km/h. He then drove another 226 km. He took 5 hours for the whole journey.

a Find the total distance Mr Patel had driven.

b What was Mr Patel's average speed for the whole journey?

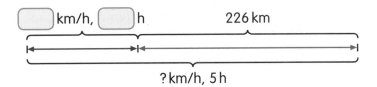

a For the first part of the journey,

Distance travelled = ⬜ × ⬜

= ⬜ km

Total distance travelled = ⬜ + ⬜

= ⬜ km

b Average speed = $\dfrac{\text{Total distance}}{\text{Total time}}$

= $\dfrac{\boxed{}}{\boxed{}}$

= ⬜ km/h

Mr Patel's average speed for the whole journey was ⬜ km/h.

5 A train travelled the first part of a journey in $1\frac{1}{2}$h. It travelled the remaining 250 km at an average speed of 100 km/h. The total distance travelled was 394 km.

a Find the total time taken for the journey.

b Find the average speed of the train for the whole journey.

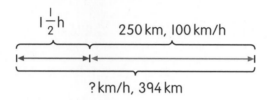

$1\frac{1}{2}$h   250 km, 100 km/h

? km/h, 394 km

a For the second part of the journey,

Time taken $= \dfrac{250}{100}$

$\qquad = 2\frac{1}{2}$h

Total time taken $= 1\frac{1}{2} + 2\frac{1}{2}$

$\qquad\qquad = 4$h

b Average speed $= \dfrac{\text{Total distance}}{\text{Total time}}$

$\qquad\qquad = \dfrac{394}{4}$

$\qquad\qquad = 98\frac{1}{2}$km/h

The average speed of the train for the whole journey was $98\frac{1}{2}$km/h.

6 📟 Farha and her mum took 3 minutes to walk from school to the shop.

They walked another 675 m at a speed of 75 m/min from the shop to the library.

They walked a total distance of 834 m.

a Find the total time taken for the journey.

b Find their average speed for the whole distance.

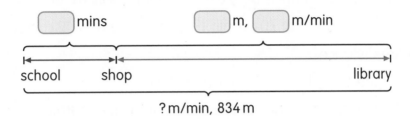

a For the second part,

Time taken = ⬭ ÷ ⬭

= ⬭ mins

Total time taken = ⬭ + ⬭

= ⬭ mins

b Average speed = $\dfrac{\text{Total distance}}{\text{Total time}}$

= $\dfrac{⬭}{⬭}$

= ⬭ m/min

Their average speed for the whole journey was ⬭ m/min.

Let's Practise!

Solve these word problems. Show your workings clearly.

7 🖩 Miya walked round a 385 m field twice. She took 5 minutes to complete the first lap and 6 minutes to complete the second lap. Find her average speed.

8 🖩 Ella walked a distance of 526 m. Then she walked for another 5 minutes at a speed of 70 m/min. She took a total of 12 minutes to walk the entire distance.

    a   Find the total distance that Ella walked.

    b   What was Ella's average speed for the whole journey?

9 🖩

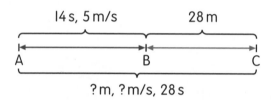

A ball rolled from Point A to Point B in 14 seconds at a speed of 5 m/s. Then it rolled a distance of 28 m from Point B to Point C. The ball took 28 seconds altogether to roll from Point A to C.

    a   Find the total distance that the ball travelled.

    b   Find the average speed of the ball.

10 A boat travelled for 4 hours from Port A to Port B. Then it travelled for 3 hours from Port B back to Port A. The distance between the two ports was 40 km.

    a   Find the total time taken for the whole journey.

    b   Find the average speed for the whole journey.

11 🖩 Mr Jackson took $1\frac{1}{3}$ h to cycle from his house to the beach. He took another $1\frac{2}{3}$ h to cycle from the beach back to his house. The distance between the house and the beach was 24 km.

    a   Find the total time taken for the whole journey.

    b   Find the average speed for the whole journey.

Practice Book 6B, p.7

Maths Journal

12 A car travels from A to B and then to C. The car takes 3 hours to travel from A to B at an average speed of 42 km/h. It travels 128 km from B to C at an average speed of 68 km/h. If the car travels for a total of 5 hours, find the average speed of the car travelling from A to C.

Ruby's answer:

> Distance = 42 + 68 = 110 km
> Speed = 110 ÷ 2 = 55 km/h
>
> The average speed of the car travelling from A to C is 55 km/h.

Hardeep's answer:

> Distance = 42 + 68 = 110 km
> Speed = 110 ÷ 5 = 22 km/h
>
> The average speed of the car travelling from A to C is 22 km/h.

Ruby and Hardeep made some mistakes in their answers. Find the mistakes and explain where they have gone wrong.

Let's Learn!

Word problems

1 Jack and Millie were standing some distance apart. Jack rolled a ball to Millie. It travelled at a speed of 30 cm/s to reach Millie in 15 seconds. Millie then rolled the ball back to Jack. It reached Jack in 10 seconds.
Find the speed of the ball as it travelled from Millie to Jack.

30 cm/s, 15 s   ? cm/s, 10 s

Jack   Millie

First find the distance between Jack and Millie.

Distance between Jack and Millie = Speed × Time
= 30 × 15
= 450 cm

Speed of ball as it rolled from Millie to Jack = Distance ÷ Time
= 450 ÷ 10
= 45 cm/s

The speed of the ball as it travelled from Millie to Jack was 45 cm/s.

2 Mr Phillips took 4 hours to drive his van from Adamstown to Berrytown at a speed of 50 km/h. On his return journey from Berrytown to Adamstown, he increased the speed to 80 km/h. How long did he take to reach Adamstown?

[   ] km/h, [   ] h

Adamstown   Berrytown

[   ] km/h, ? h

First find the distance between Adamstown and Berrytown.

Distance between Adamstown and Berrytown = [   ] × [   ]
= [   ] km

Time taken to reach Adamstown from Berrytown = [   ] ÷ [   ]
= [   ] h

Mr Phillips took h to reach Adamstown.

3 📟 Mrs Jones was travelling from Claireville to Appleyard. She took 2 hours to drive $\frac{1}{4}$ of the journey. She drove the remaining 270 km in 3 hours.

a Find the total distance that Mrs Jones drove.

b Find the average speed for the whole journey.

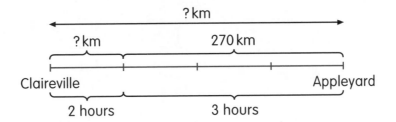

a 3 units ⟶ 270 km

I unit ⟶ $\frac{270}{3}$

= 90 km

4 units ⟶ 4 × 90

= 360 km

The total distance that Mrs Jones drove was 360 km.

b Total time taken for the whole journey = 2 + 3

= 5 h

Average speed for the whole journey = $\dfrac{\text{Total distance}}{\text{Total time}}$

= $\dfrac{\boxed{}}{\boxed{}}$

= 72 km/h

The average speed for the whole journey was 72 km/h.

4 Sophie cycled from her house to the park. She took 4 minutes to cycle $\frac{1}{3}$ of the distance and took another 12 minutes to cycle the remaining 1584 m.

a Find the distance between Sophie's house and the park.

b Find her average speed for the whole journey.

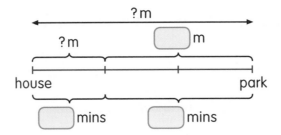

a 2 units ⟶ ☐ m

1 unit ⟶ ☐ ÷ 2

= ☐ m

3 units ⟶ 3 × ☐

= ☐ m

The distance between Sophie's house and the park was ☐ m.

b Total time taken for the whole distance = ☐ + ☐

= ☐ mins

Average speed for the whole journey = $\dfrac{\text{Total distance}}{\text{Total time}}$

= $\dfrac{\boxed{}}{\boxed{}}$

= ☐ m/min

Her average speed for the whole journey was ☐ m/min.

5   Tai took 30 minutes to run a distance of 3600 m from A to C.

He took 5 minutes to run from A to B, which is $\frac{1}{5}$ of the total distance.

What was his average speed for the remaining distance?

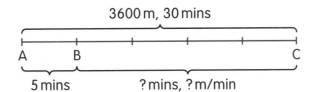

5 units ⟶ 3600 m

1 unit ⟶ $\frac{3600}{5}$

       = 720 m

4 units ⟶ 4 × 720

       = 2880 m

Distance between B and C = 2880 m

Time taken to run from B to C = 30 − 5

                             = 25 mins

Average speed for the remaining distance = $\dfrac{\text{Distance}}{\text{Time}}$

                                             = $\dfrac{2880}{25}$

                                             = $115\frac{1}{5}$ m/min

His average speed for the remaining distance was $115\frac{1}{5}$ m/min.

Home Maths   Help your child to find the average speeds of other journeys such as their walk to school, the bus journey into town or a drive to visit relatives.

6 A lorry travelled for 5 hours from Factory A to Factory C, via Factory B, at an average speed of 64 km/h. It travelled from Factory B to Factory C at an average speed of 80 km/h. If the distance between Factory A and Factory B is $\frac{1}{4}$ of the total distance between Factory A and Factory C, how long did the lorry take to travel from Factory B to Factory C?

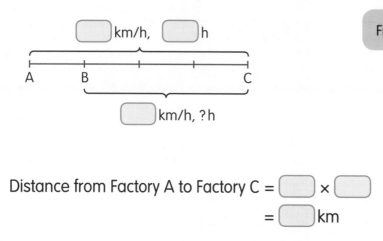

First find the total distance.

Distance from Factory A to Factory C = ☐ × ☐
= ☐ km

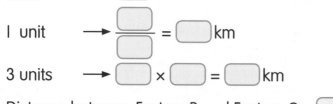

☐ units ⟶ ☐ km

1 unit ⟶ $\dfrac{☐}{☐}$ = ☐ km

3 units ⟶ ☐ × ☐ = ☐ km

Distance between Factory B and Factory C = ☐ km

Time taken to travel from Factory B to Factory C = ☐ ÷ ☐ = ☐ h

The lorry took ☐ h to travel from Factory B to Factory C.

Activity

7 Draw diagrams to show the following.

a Omar and his dad walked from their home to the swimming pool at an average speed of $4\frac{1}{2}$ km/h for $\frac{1}{2}$ h. Then they walked back home at an average speed of $3\frac{4}{5}$ km/h.

b Mr Lee took 20 minutes to walk from Point A to Point B over a distance of 760 m. He took 4 minutes to run $\frac{1}{5}$ of the journey.

Let's Practise!

Solve these word problems. Show your workings clearly.

8 Mr Campbell drove for 5 hours from Oxford to Leeds at an average speed of 60 km/h. How long would it take to travel the same distance if Mr Campbell drove at an average speed of 80 km/h?

9 Miya took 20 seconds to run from Point A to Point B at a speed of 4·5 m/s. She took 18 seconds to run back from Point B to Point A. Find Miya's average speed when she ran from Point B to Point A.

10 Mrs Anderson took 1 hour to drive $\frac{1}{5}$ of a journey from Thatchville to Waterlake. She drove the remaining 180 km in 4 hours.

a What was Mrs Anderson's speed for the first part of the journey?

b How long did she take to travel the whole journey?

c Find Mrs Anderson's average speed for the whole journey.

Let's Practise!

11 Hannah took 30 minutes to cycle from her house to the cinema. If she cycled the first 3 km of the journey at a speed of 150 m/min, find her average speed for the remaining 3 km of the journey.

12 Mr Bell took a total of 4 hours to drive from Jamestown to Simonstown. He took 1 hour to travel from Jamestown to Hollyville, which is between Jamestown and Simonstown. The distance between Hollyville and Simonstown is $\frac{11}{15}$ of the distance between Jamestown and Simonstown. If the total distance travelled is 360 km, find Mr Bell's speed for the journey from Hollyville to Simonstown.

13 Mr Roberts drove a distance of 118 km from London to Southampton. At first he drove at a speed of 60 km/h. Then he drove for $1\frac{1}{4}$ h to Southampton, covering a distance of 70 km. If Mr Roberts left London at 14:00, what time did he arrive at Southampton?

> Practice Book 6B, p.11

Let's Wrap It Up!

You have learnt to:

- calculate speed, distance or time given the other 2 quantities
- use the formulae:
    - **Speed = Distance ÷ Time**
    - **Distance = Speed × Time**
    - **Time = Distance ÷ Speed**
- find average speed
- read, interpret and write speed in different units: km/h, m/min, m/s and cm/s
- draw diagrams to solve word problems about speed.

Let's Wrap It Up!

Let's Revise!

14 Ruby's mum took $1\frac{1}{2}$ h to travel from Oxford to London at an average speed of 56 km/h. She parked for $\frac{3}{10}$ h in London. On her return journey, she increased her average speed to 70 km/h.

$$1\frac{1}{2}\text{h, 56 km/h} \qquad\qquad 70\text{ km/h}$$

Oxford   London

?h

a Find the distance between Oxford and London.

Distance between Oxford and London $= 1\frac{1}{2} \times 56$

$= 84\,\text{km}$

b Find the time taken on the return journey.

Time taken from London to Oxford $= 84 \div 70$

$= 1\frac{1}{5}\text{h}$

c Find her total time taken for the whole journey.

Total time taken for the whole journey $= 1\frac{1}{2} + 1\frac{1}{5} + \frac{3}{10}$

$= 3\,\text{h}$

Put On Your Thinking Caps!

15 Millie and Hardeep cycled 3·5 km from the school to the library along the same route. When Millie arrived at the library at 11:15, Hardeep was 1·5 km away from the library. If Hardeep cycled at an average speed of 15 km/h, what time did he leave the school?

Practice Book 6B, p.16 Practice Book 6B, p.18

8 Circles

Let's Learn!

> ## Radius, diameter and circumference

Radius

 These are circles.

A circle can be drawn with a pair of compasses.

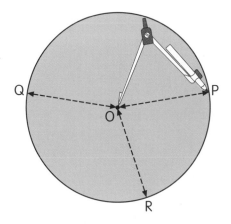

O is the **centre** of the circle.
OP is a **radius** of the circle.
OQ and OR are also **radii** of the circle.
OP = OQ = OR

 Radii of a circle are equal.

2   Use a pair of compasses to draw a circle and label its centre O. Draw 4 radii of the circle and label them OA, OB, OC and OD. Measure each radius in centimetres to I decimal place. What can you say about OA, OB, OC and OD?

3   Draw a circle with a radius of 5 cm.

Step I

Measure 5 cm on a ruler with a pair of compasses.

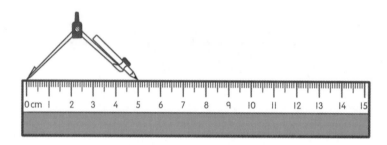

Step 2

Draw the circle.

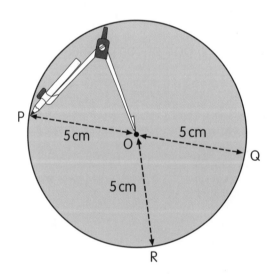

4   Draw a circle with a radius of:

a   4 cm   **b**   6 cm.

Label the centre O. For each circle, draw the radii OP and OQ so that PQ is a straight line through the centre O. What is the length of PQ for each circle?

Diameter

5 In the diagram below, O is the centre of the circle. The lines PQ and RS pass through the centre. PQ is a **diameter** of the circle. RS is another diameter of the circle. TU is not a diameter.

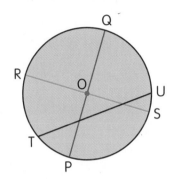

Diameters of a circle pass through its centre.

OP and OQ are radii of the circle.
OP = OQ
PQ = 2 × OP or PQ = 2 × OQ

Diameter = 2 × Radius
Radius = Diameter ÷ 2

6 **a** **i** In the diagram, O is the centre of the circle. Name the diameters.

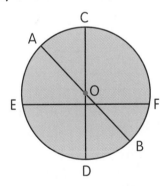

ii Which line is not a diameter? Explain.

b The radius of a circle is 6 cm. What is the length of its diameter?

c The diameter of a circle is 15 cm. What is the length of its radius?

Practice Book 6B, p.19

31

Circilcumference
Circumference

7

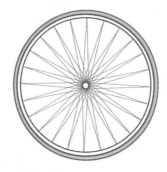

The circumference of a circle is its perimeter.

A bicycle wheel has the shape of a circle.
The distance around the wheel is called its circumference.

Activity

8 Tai uses a piece of string to measure the circumference of each circle to I decimal place and records it in the table below. Copy the table, divide the circumference of each circle by its diameter to I decimal place, and fill in the answers. What do you notice?

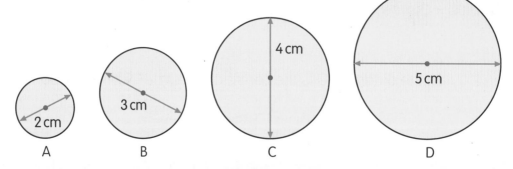

A   B   C   D

Circle	Diameter	Circumference	Circumference ÷ Diameter
A	2 cm	6·2 cm	
B	3 cm	9·4 cm	
C	4 cm	12·5 cm	
D	5 cm	15·6 cm	

The circumference of any circle divided by its diameter always has the same value. This number is called π.

Activity

To see the value of π on your calculator, press: $\boxed{\pi}$ $\boxed{=}$

Give the value of π to:

a   I decimal place

b   2 decimal places

c   3 decimal places.

π is a Greek letter. We read it as pi.

We usually take the value of π to be **3·14** or $\frac{22}{7}$.

Since circumference ÷ diameter = π,

Circumference = π × Diameter

Circumference of a pie = pi × Diameter of pie

I can find the circumference of a circle when I know its diameter.

Can you find the circumference of a circle if you know the radius?

9   The radius of a circular plate is 10·5 cm. Find its circumference. $\left(\text{Take } \pi = \frac{22}{7}\right)$

Diameter of plate = 2 × Radius
$$= 2 \times 10·5$$
$$= 21 \text{ cm}$$

Circumference of plate = π × Diameter
$$= \frac{22}{7} \times 21$$
$$= 66 \text{ cm}$$

Home Maths

Explain that the diameter of an object with a circular face can be measured in this way. Draw around the base of the object on a piece of paper and fold the circle in half to find the diameter. Ask your child to measure the diameter to the nearest centimetre of similiar objects like this and find the circumference of the circular face of each object.

10 The diameter of a bicycle wheel is 55 cm. Find the circumference of the wheel. (Take π = 3·14)

$$\text{Circumference of wheel} = \pi \times \text{Diameter}$$
$$= 3\cdot14 \times 55$$
$$= 172\cdot7 \, \text{cm}$$

11 The diameter of a circular track is 127 m. Find its circumference to 2 decimal places.

Circumference of track
$= \pi \times \text{Diameter}$
$= \pi \times 127$
$\approx 398\cdot98 \, \text{m}$

Press	Display
C	0
π	π
× 1 2 7	127
=	398.982267

12 Taking $\pi = \frac{22}{7}$, find the circumference of a circle of with a:

a   14 cm diameter

b   21 cm radius.

13 Taking π = 3·14, find the circumference of a circle of with a:

a   25 cm diameter

b   16 cm radius.

14 Find the circumference of each circle. Give your answer to 1 decimal place.

a   Diameter = 44 cm

b   Radius = 31·5 cm

If the value of π is not given, use the π button on your calculator.

15 Ella folds a paper circle in half. Then she unfolds the paper circle.

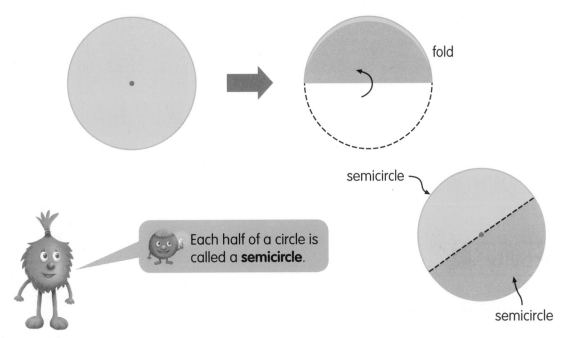

fold

semicircle

semicircle

Each half of a circle is called a **semicircle**.

16 Jack folds a paper circle in quarters. Then he unfolds the paper circle.

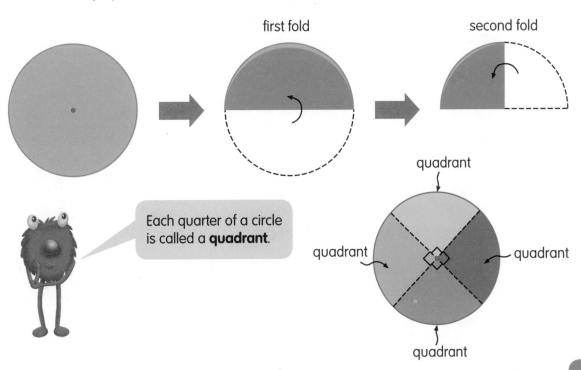

first fold

second fold

quadrant

quadrant

quadrant

quadrant

Each quarter of a circle is called a **quadrant**.

17 The circumference of a circle with a 7 cm radius is 44 cm. What is the perimeter of:

a   a semicircle?   **b**   a quadrant?

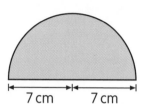

7 cm   7 cm

7 cm

Practice Book 6B, p.23

Activity

18 Work in pairs.

a   Using a pair of compasses, draw a circle with a 6 cm radius on a piece of paper. Label the centre O. Draw a diameter of the circle. Label it PQ. What do you notice?

A diameter of the circle cuts it into ⬚ semicircles.

This shape is made up of one of the semicircles and the diameter PQ of the circle. Find its perimeter. (Take $\pi = 3.14$)

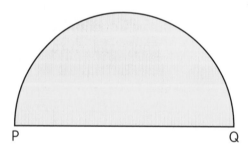

P   Q

b   In the circle in **a**, draw another diameter perpendicular to PQ. Label it RS. What do you notice?

Two perpendicular diameters of the circle cut it into ⬚ quadrants.

Activity

c   This shape shows one of the quadrants and the radii OQ and OR of the circle. Find its perimeter. (Take $\pi = 3.14$)

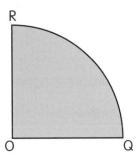

d   This shape is made up of one semicircle, one quadrant and the radii OQ and OR of the circle. Find its perimeter. (Take $\pi = 3.14$)

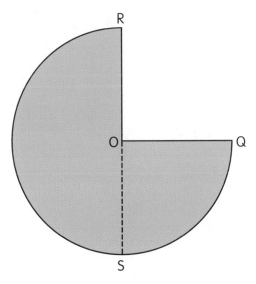

19 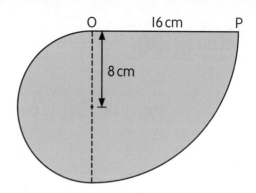 The shape is made up of a semicircle and a quadrant. Find the perimeter of the shape. (Take $\pi = 3.14$)

Perimeter of shape = Length of semicircle curve + Length of quadrant curve + OP

Length of semicircle curve = $\dfrac{\text{Circumference of circle}}{2}$

$= \dfrac{\pi \times 16}{2}$

$= 3.14 \times 8$

$= 25.12 \text{ cm}$

Length of quadrant curve = $\dfrac{\text{Circumference of circle}}{4}$

$= \dfrac{\pi \times 32}{4}$

$= 3.14 \times 8$

$= 25.12 \text{ cm}$

Length of OP = 16 cm

Perimeter of shape = 25.12 + 25.12 + 16
$= 66.24 \text{ cm}$

20 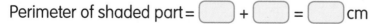 The shape is made up of a semicircle and a quadrant. Find the perimeter of the shaded part. (Take $\pi = 3.14$)

Perimeter of shaded part = Length of semicircle curve + OQ

Length of semicircle curve = ⬚ × ⬚

$=$ ⬚ cm

OQ = ⬚ cm

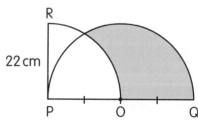

Perimeter of shaded part = ⬚ + ⬚ = ⬚ cm

Let's Practise!

21 In the diagram, O is the centre of the circle and AB is a straight line.

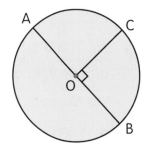

a OA, OB and OC are ⬚ of the circle.

b AB is a ⬚ of the circle.

c OA = ⬚ = ⬚

d AB = ⬚ × OC

e Circumference of the circle = $\pi \times$ ⬚

22 Find the circumference of each circle. $\left(\text{Take } \pi = \frac{22}{7}\right)$

a

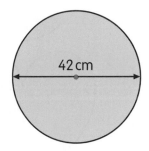

42 cm

b

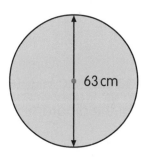

63 cm

c

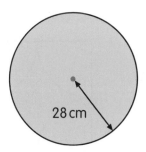

28 cm

d

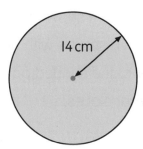

14 cm

23 🖩 Find the circumference of each circle. Give your answer to 1 decimal place. (Take $\pi = 3\cdot14$)

a Diameter = 13 cm

b Diameter = 16 cm

c Radius = 11·5 cm

d Radius = 5·5 cm

Let's Practise!

24 The cover of a tin of paint is a circle with a diameter of 20 cm. Find the circumference of the cover. (Take $\pi = 3\cdot14$)

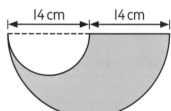

25 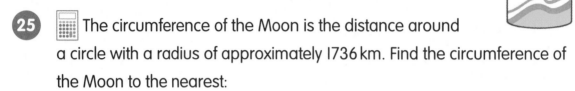 The circumference of the Moon is the distance around a circle with a radius of approximately 1736 km. Find the circumference of the Moon to the nearest:

a ten kilometres

b thousand kilometres.

$\left(\text{Take } \pi = \dfrac{22}{7}\right)$

26 The diagram shows two semicircles. Find the perimeter of the shaded part. $\left(\text{Take } \pi = \dfrac{22}{7}\right)$

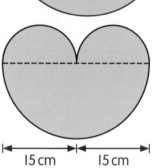

14 cm   14 cm

27 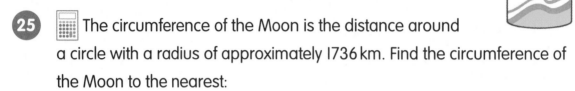 The diagram shows three semicircles. Find the perimeter of the diagram. (Take $\pi = 3\cdot14$)

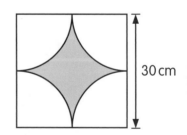

15 cm   15 cm

28 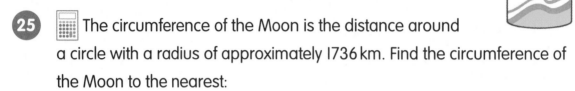 The diagram shows four identical quadrants enclosed in a square with 30 cm sides. Find the perimeter of the shaded part. Give your answer to 2 decimal places.

30 cm

29 The diagram shows two identical quadrants. Find the perimeter of the shaded part. $\left(\text{Take } \pi = \dfrac{22}{7}\right)$

14 cm

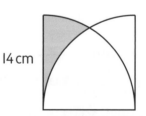

Practice Book 6B, p.27

Let's Learn!

Area of a circle

1

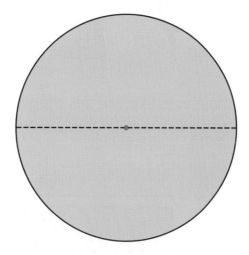

A diameter cuts a circle into 2 semicircles.
Since circumference = $\pi \times$ Diameter,

Length of semicircle curve $= \dfrac{\pi \times \text{Diameter}}{2}$

$= \pi \times \dfrac{\text{Diameter}}{2}$

$= \pi \times \text{Radius}$

2 Farha draws a circle as shown below.

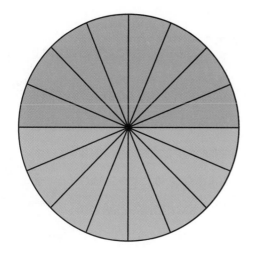

How many diameters has Farha drawn?

She cuts the circle into 16 equal pieces.

She cuts one of the pieces into two equal pieces and draws stripes on them.

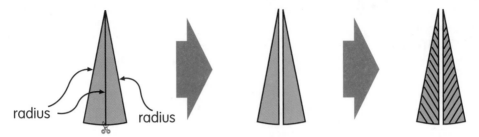

radius — radius

She then arranges all the pieces to make this shape.

Each semicircle makes the top and bottom of this shape.

length of semicircle curve

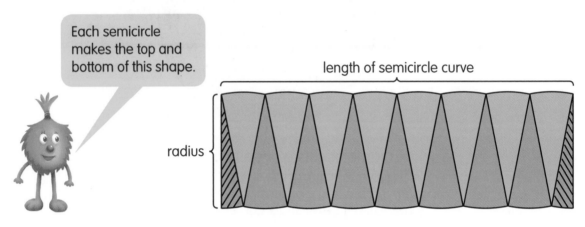

radius

Area of the circle = Area of the above shape

Imagine Farha cuts the circle into a very, very large number of equal pieces so that each piece is very, very narrow. When the number of pieces is as large as can be and they are arranged as above, this shape will be formed.

$\pi \times$ radius

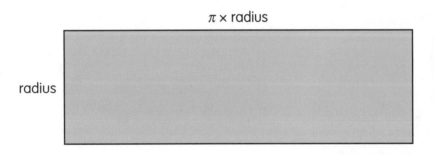

radius

The shape becomes a rectangle. What is the length and width of this rectangle?

Area of circle = Area of rectangle
= Length × Width
= $\pi \times$ Radius × Radius

Area of circle = $\pi \times$ Radius × Radius

3 Find the area of a circle with a radius of 12 cm. (Take $\pi = 3\cdot14$)

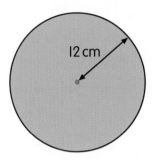

12 cm

Area of circle = $\pi \times$ Radius $\times$ Radius
$= 3\cdot14 \times 12 \times 12$
$= 452\cdot16 \text{ cm}^2$

4 The diameter of a circular disc is 18 cm. Find the area of the disc in terms of π.

Radius of disc = $18 \div 2$
$= 9 \text{ cm}$

Area of disc = $\pi \times 9 \times 9$
$= \pi \times 81$
$= 81\,\pi \text{ cm}^2$

5 Find the area of each circle. (Take $\pi = 3\cdot14$)

a Radius = 12 cm

b Radius = 15 cm

c Diameter = 26 cm

Activity

6   **a**   With a pair of compasses, draw a circle with a radius of 5 cm on I cm
square grid paper as shown.

b   Mark the two perpendicular diameters (in red) clearly on your diagram.

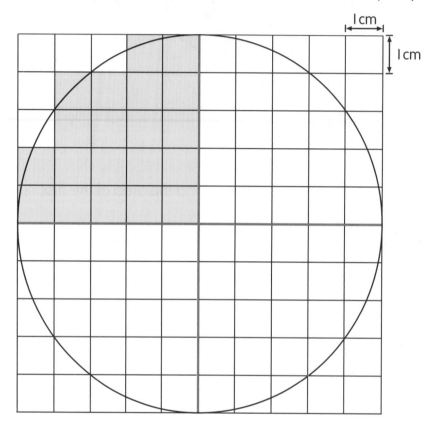

1 cm

1 cm

c   Count the number of squares in the top left quadrant:
  • More than half squares are counted as whole squares.
  • Less than half squares are not counted.

What is the area of the quadrant?
Use your answer to find the area of the circle.

d   Taking $\pi = 3.14$, find the area of the circle using the formula:

$$\text{Area} = \pi \times \text{Radius} \times \text{Radius}$$

Do the two methods give the same area?
Which method do you think gives a more accurate answer?

7 🖩 The shape below is made up of a semicircle and two identical quadrants. Find the area of the shaded part. (Take π = 3·14)

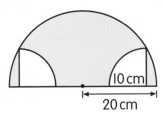

Area of shaded part = Area of semicircle – 2 × Area of quadrant

$$= \frac{1}{2} \times 3\cdot14 \times 20 \times 20 - 2 \times \frac{1}{4} \times 3\cdot14 \times 10 \times 10$$

$$= 628 - 157$$

$$= 471 \, cm^2$$

8 The shape below is made up of a quadrant and two semicircles. Find the area of the shape. $\left(\text{Take } \pi = \frac{22}{7}\right)$

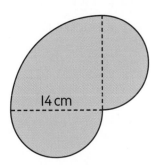

14 cm

Area of shape = Area of quadrant + 2 × Area of semicircle

Area of shape = ☐ × ☐ × ☐ × ☐ + ☐ × ☐ × ☐ × ☐ × ☐

= ☐ + ☐

= ☐ cm²

Let's Practise!

9 Find the area of each circle. (Take $\pi = 3 \cdot 14$)

a

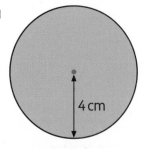

4 cm

b

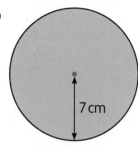

7 cm

c

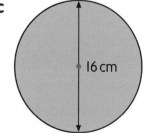

16 cm

d

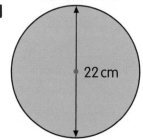

22 cm

10 Taking $\pi = \dfrac{22}{7}$, find the area of each semicircle.

a

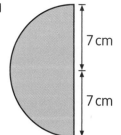

7 cm

7 cm

b

14 cm 14 cm

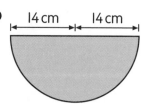

11 Calculate the area of each quadrant. Give your answer to 1 decimal place.

a

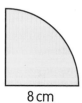

8 cm

b

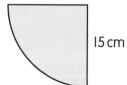

15 cm

Let's Practise!

12 O is the centre of the big circle and OA is a diameter of the small circle. Find the area of the shaded part in terms of π.

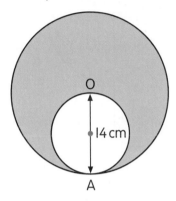

14 cm

13 🖩 O is the centre of the big circle and AB is its diameter. Two smaller semicircles are enclosed within the big circle as shown. If AB = 28 cm, find the area of the shaded part. $\left(\text{Take } \pi = \frac{22}{7}\right)$

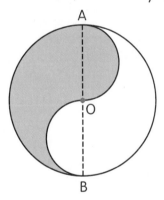

14 🖩 This shape shows three semicircles. Taking $\pi = 3.14$, find the area of the shaded part.

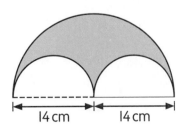

14 cm   14 cm

Let's Practise!

15 The shape below is made up of a semicircle and a quadrant. Find the area of the shape. (Take $\pi = 3\cdot14$)

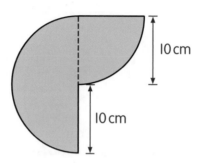

10 cm

10 cm

16 The shape below is made up of two quadrants. Find the area of the shape. Give your answer to 2 decimal places.

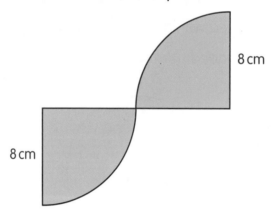

8 cm

8 cm

17 The shape below is made up of three quadrants. Find the area of the shape. $\left(\text{Take } \pi = \dfrac{22}{7}\right)$

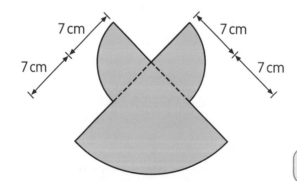

7 cm   7 cm

7 cm   7 cm

Practice Book 6B, p.33

Maths Journal

18 Find the circumference and area of a circle with a diameter of 8 cm.
Give your answer to 1 decimal place.

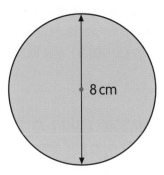

8 cm

Ruby's answers are:

> Circumference of circle = 50·3 cm
>
> Area of circle = 201·1 cm²

By estimating, explain why Ruby's answers are not reasonable.

Let's Wrap It Up!

You have learnt to:

- identify and name the centre, radii, diameters and circumference of a circle
- recognise a semicircle as half a circle and a quadrant as a quarter of a circle
- state that the circumference of a circle is equal to $\pi \times$ Diameter
- state that the area of a circle is equal to $\pi \times$ Radius $\times$ Radius.

Let's Revise!

 19 This diagram shows a circle with centre O.
PQ is a diameter and OP, OQ and OR are
radii of the circle.

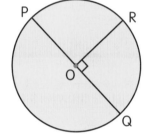

a OP = OQ = OR

b PQ = 2 × OP

c Circumference of circle = $\pi \times$ PQ = 2 × π × OP

d Length of semicircle curve = $\pi \times \dfrac{PQ}{2}$ = π × OP

e Length of quadrant curve = $\pi \times \dfrac{PQ}{4}$ = $\pi \times \dfrac{OP}{2}$

f Area of circle = π × OP × OP

g Area of semicircle = π × OP × $\dfrac{OP}{2}$

h Area of quadrant = π × OP × $\dfrac{OP}{4}$

Let's Wrap It Up!

20 This diagram shows a semicircle and a quadrant.
Find the perimeter and area of the shaded part.

$\left(\text{Take } \pi = \dfrac{22}{7}\right)$

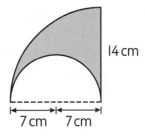

14 cm

7 cm   7 cm

Perimeter of shaded part = Length of semicircle curve +
Length of quadrant curve + 14 cm

$$= \frac{1}{2} \times \frac{22}{7} \times 14 + \frac{1}{4} \times \frac{22}{7} \times 28 + 14$$

$$= 22 + 22 + 14$$

$$= 58 \text{ cm}$$

Area of shaded part = Area of quadrant – Area of semicircle

$$= \frac{1}{4} \times \frac{22}{7} \times 14 \times 14 - \frac{1}{2} \times \frac{22}{7} \times 7 \times 7$$

$$= 154 - 77$$

$$= 77 \text{ cm}^2$$

Put On Your Thinking Caps!

21 The distance covered by a bicycle wheel when it does one complete turn is AB. If the diameter of the wheel is 56 cm, find in metres the distance covered in 500 complete turns of the wheel. $\left(\text{Take } \pi = \frac{22}{7}\right)$

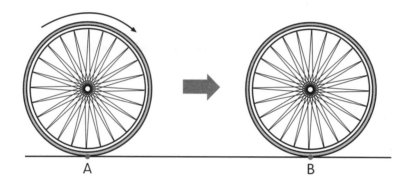

A   B

22 The diagram below shows a circle with a radius of 7 cm and four identical quadrants. Find the total area of the shaded parts. $\left(\text{Take } \pi = \frac{22}{7}\right)$

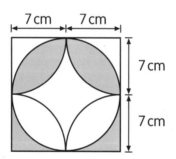

7 cm | 7 cm

7 cm

7 cm

Practice Book 6B, p.45

Unit 9 Pie Charts

Let's Learn!

Understanding pie charts

1 About 70% of the Earth's surface is water. The remaining 30% of the Earth's surface is land. We can show this fact in a table.

Earth's Surface	100%
Water	70%
Land	30%

We can also show this in a graph called a **pie chart**.

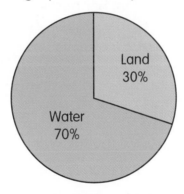

$70\% + 30\% = 100\%$

The whole circle is always 100%.

2 The pie chart below shows the percentage of boys in a school. What percentage of the pupils are girls?

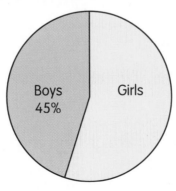

3 This pie chart shows how Miya spends her monthly pocket money.

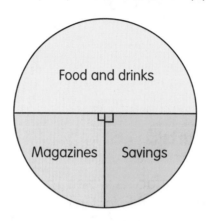

a From the pie chart, we can tell that Miya:

- spends $\frac{1}{2}$ of her pocket money on food and drinks,

- spends $\frac{1}{4}$ of her pocket money on magazines, and

- saves the remaining $\frac{1}{4}$ of her pocket money.

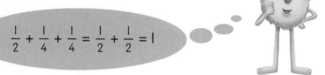

$$\frac{1}{2} + \frac{1}{4} + \frac{1}{4} = \frac{1}{2} + \frac{1}{2} = 1$$

b If Miya gets £10 a month:

   i how much of her pocket money does she spend on food and drinks?

   ii how much of her pocket money does she save?

   iii how much more does she spend on food and drinks than on magazines?

   i $\frac{1}{2} \times £10 = £5$

      She spends £5·00 of her pocket money on food and drinks.

   ii $\frac{1}{4} \times £10 = £2·50$

      She saves £2·50.

   iii   Amount of money she spends on magazines = Amount of savings
                                               = £2·50

      £5 − £2·50 = £2·50
      She spends £2·50 more on food and drinks than on magazines.

4 This pie chart shows how another pupil, Ella, spends her monthly pocket money of £15.

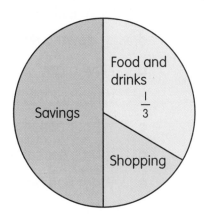

a What fraction of her pocket money does she save?

b What fraction of her pocket money does she spend on shopping?

c How much of her pocket money does she spend on food and drinks?

d How much of her pocket money does she save?

5 Among 75 pupils, 15 pupils have fish as pets, 25 pupils have a cat, 18 pupils have a hamster and the rest don't have any pets. The pie chart here shows this information.

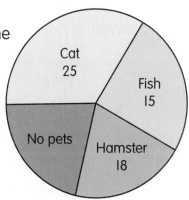

a How many pupils don't have any pets?

b What fraction of the pupils have fish?

c What fraction of the pupils have a cat?

d What percentage of the pupils have a hamster?

a $75 - (15 + 25 + 18) = 17$

17 pupils don't have any pets.

b $\dfrac{15}{75} = \dfrac{1}{5}$

$\dfrac{1}{5}$ of the pupils have fish.

c $\dfrac{25}{75} = \dfrac{1}{3}$

$\dfrac{1}{3}$ of the pupils have a cat.

d $\dfrac{18}{75} \times 100\% = \dfrac{18 \times 100}{75} \%$

$\qquad = 24\%$

24% of the pupils have a hamster.

6 This pie chart shows the number of vehicles driving down a street one morning.

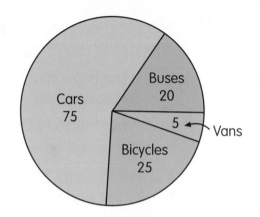

a How many vehicles are there altogether?

b What fraction of the vehicles are cars?

c What fraction of the vehicles are bicycles?

d What percentage of the vehicles are buses?

e What percentage of the vehicles are vans?

Activity

7 Work in pairs.

I Look at the pie chart below. Think of a question for your partner to answer.

2 Take turns doing this.

3 Ask as many questions as you can.

The pie chart shows how a pupil spends his time during the 24 hours of a day.

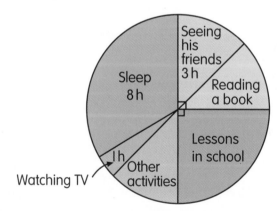

Example

How many hours does the pupil spend on lessons in school?
What fraction of the day does he spend sleeping?

Let's Practise!

8 The following pie chart shows the types of fruit Mrs O'Carroll sold one Monday morning.

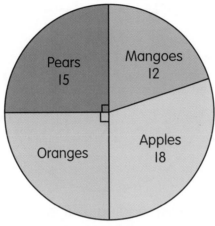

a Which type of fruit did she sell the most?

b How many oranges did she sell?

c How many more apples than oranges did she sell?

d How many pieces of fruit did she sell altogether?

9 This pie chart shows the attendance at a school concert.

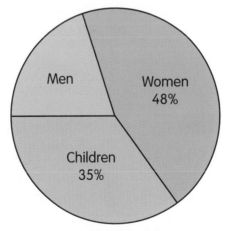

a What percentage of the audience were women and children?

b What percentage of the audience were men?

c If there were 280 children at the concert, how many women were there?

Let's Practise!

10 This pie chart shows the favourite hobbies listed by a group of 84 children.

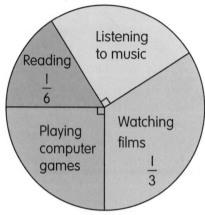

a How many children list reading as their hobby?

b How many children list listening to music as their hobby?

c What fraction of the children list playing computer games as their hobby?

d Which hobby is twice as popular as another?

11 This pie chart shows the results of matches played by the leading team in a football league.

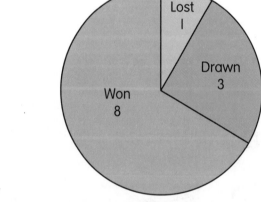

a How many matches did the team play?

b What fraction of the matches did the team win?

c What fraction of the matches ended in a draw?

d If 3 points were awarded for a win, 1 point for a draw and 0 points for a loss, how many points did the team score?

Let's Practise!

12 This pie chart shows how a group of people travel to work.

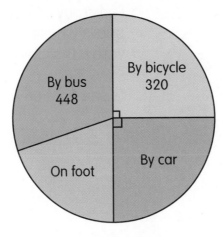

a How many people travel to work by car?

b What fraction of the people travel to work by bicycle?

c How many people travel to work by bicycle or by car?

d How many people walk to work?

e What percentage of the people travel to work by bus?

13 This pie chart shows how Mr Robinson spends his monthly salary.

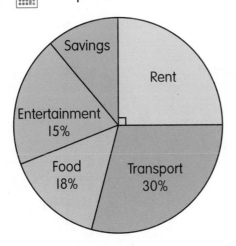

a What percentage of his salary is spent on rent?

b What percentage of his salary does he save?

c If he saves £450 a month:

   i how much is his salary?

   ii how much does he spend on entertainment and transport a month?

Practice Book 6B, pp.47 and 57

Maths Journal

14 This pie chart shows the favourite colours of a class of pupils.

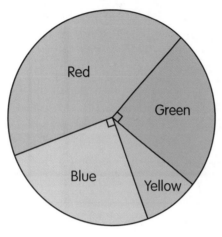

Farha says that the total percentage of pupils whose favourite colour is red or yellow is slightly more than 50%.

Is she right or wrong? Why?

Let's Wrap It Up!

You have learnt to:

- recognise that a pie chart is another kind of graph
- recognise that the whole circle represents 100% or 1 whole
- read and interpret pie charts.

Let's Revise!

15 This pie chart shows the different colours of straws in a pack.

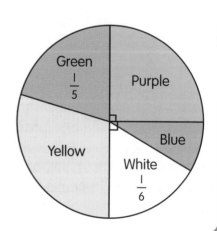

a What fraction of the straws are yellow? $\frac{3}{10}$

b What fraction of the straws are blue? $\frac{1}{12}$

c What percentage of the straws are **not** purple? 75%

d What percentage of the straws are **not** yellow or green? 50%

Put On Your Thinking Caps!

16 This pie chart shows the activities outside school that some pupils in a school take part in. Each pupil takes part in only one activity.

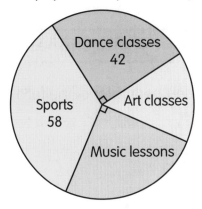

a What fraction of the pupils take part in dance classes?

b What percentage of the pupils have music lessons?

c How many pupils are there altogether?

d How many pupils take part in art classes?

e What is the ratio of the total number of pupils taking part in sports to the total number of pupils?

Practice Book 6B, p.65

Unit 10 — Area and Perimeter

Let's Learn!

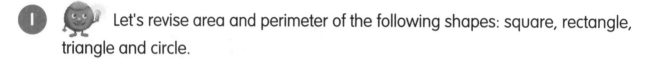

Area and perimeter of composite shapes

1 Let's revise area and perimeter of the following shapes: square, rectangle, triangle and circle.

This square has 6 cm sides.

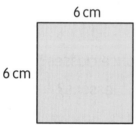

6 cm

6 cm

> Perimeter of closed polygon with straight sides = Sum of its sides

> Area of square = Length × Width
>
> A square has the same length and width.

Perimeter = ☐ × ☐

= ☐ cm

Area = ☐ × ☐

= ☐ cm²

2 This rectangle is 9 cm long and 7 cm wide.

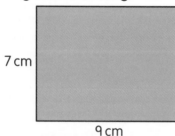

7 cm

9 cm

> Area of rectangle = Length × Width

Perimeter = ☐ + ☐ + ☐ + ☐

= ☐ cm

Area = ☐ × ☐

= ☐ cm²

3 This triangle has 13 cm, 13 cm and 10 cm sides, and a height of 12 cm.

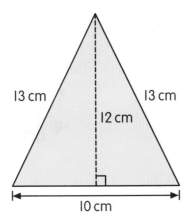

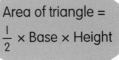

Area of triangle =
$\frac{1}{2}$ × Base × Height

Perimeter = ☐ + ☐ + ☐
= ☐ cm

Area = ☐ × ☐ × ☐
= ☐ cm²

4 This circle has a radius of 7 cm. $\left(\text{Take } \pi = \frac{22}{7}\right)$

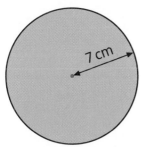

Circumference of circle =
π × Diameter

Area of circle =
π × Radius × Radius

Circumference = π × ☐
= ☐ cm

Area = π × ☐ × ☐
= ☐ cm²

Practice Book 6B, p.85

5 Find the area and perimeter of the shape.

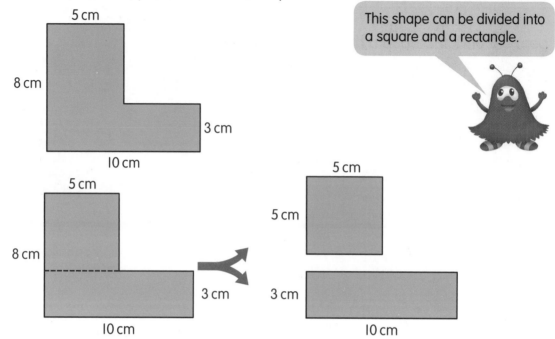

This shape can be divided into a square and a rectangle.

Side of square = 5 cm
Area of square = 5 × 5
= 25 cm²

Area of rectangle = 10 × 3
= 30 cm²

Area of shape = 25 + 30
= 55 cm²

Method I

Perimeter of shape = 8 + 10 + 3 + 5 + 5 + 5
= 36 cm

Method 2

Perimeter of shape = 8 + 10 + 8 + 10
= 36 cm

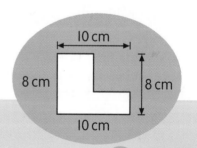

Home Maths — Ask your child to work out the area of your bathroom tiles or carpet, using a tape measure.

6 Find the area and perimeter of this trapezium.

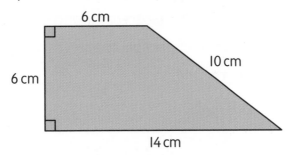

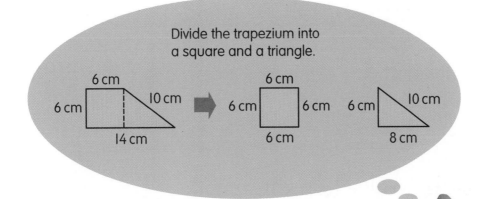

Divide the trapezium into a square and a triangle.

Area of square = ☐ × ☐
= ☐ cm²

Area of triangle = ☐ × ☐ × ☐
= ☐ cm²

Area of trapezium = ☐ + ☐
= ☐ cm²

Perimeter of trapezium = ☐ + ☐ + ☐ + ☐
= ☐ cm

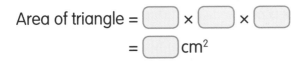

Practice Book 6B, p.87

7 This shape is made up of a square with 32 cm sides, an isosceles triangle and a quadrant. The height of the isosceles triangle is 12 cm and each equal side is 20 cm long. Find the area and perimeter of the shape. Give your answer to 1 decimal place. (Take $\pi = 3.14$)

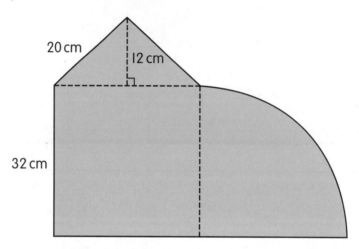

Area of isosceles triangle = $\frac{1}{2} \times 12 \times 32$
$= 192 \, cm^2$

Area of square = 32×32
$= 1024 \, cm^2$

Area of quadrant = $\frac{1}{4} \times 3.14 \times 32 \times 32$
$= 803.84 \, cm^2$

Area of shape = $192 + 1024 + 803.84$
$= 2019.8 \, cm^2$

Length of quadrant curve = $\frac{1}{4} \times 3.14 \times 2 \times 32$
$= 50.24 \, cm$

Perimeter of shape = $20 + 20 + 32 + 32 + 32 + 50.24$
$= 186.2 \, cm$

8 This diagram shows two semicircles in a rectangle 40 cm by 32 cm.
Find the area and perimeter of the shaded part. Give your answer to
2 decimal places.

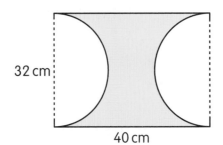

32 cm

40 cm

Area of rectangle = 40 × 32
= 1280 cm²

Area of the two semicircles = Area of circle
= π × 16 × 16
≈ 804·248 cm²

Area of shaded part = 1280 − 804·248
≈ 475·75 cm²

Length of the two semicircle curves = Circumference of circle
= π × 32
≈ 100·531 cm

Perimeter of shaded part = 100·531 + 40 + 40
≈ 180·53 cm

9 This diagram shows two quadrants in a square with 12 cm sides. Find the area
and perimeter of the shaded part. $\left(\text{Take } \pi = \dfrac{22}{7}\right)$

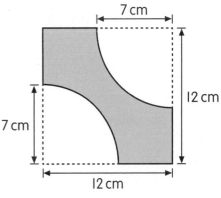

7 cm

7 cm

12 cm

12 cm

Area of square = ⬚ × ⬚ = ⬚ cm²

Area of the two quadrants
= Area of semicircle
= ⬚ × ⬚ × ⬚ × ⬚
= ⬚ cm²

Area of shaded part = ⬚ − ⬚
= ⬚ cm²

Length of the two quadrant curves = Length of semicircle curve
= ⬚ × ⬚ × ⬚
= ⬚ cm

Perimeter of shaded part = ⬚ + ⬚ + ⬚ + ⬚ + ⬚
= ⬚ cm

Let's Explore!

10 Work in pairs:

I Draw the rectangle and square on a piece of paper and cut them out.

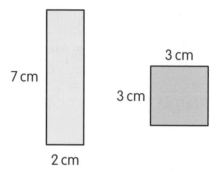

7 cm

2 cm

3 cm

3 cm

2 With the rectangle and the square, make these three types of composite shapes.

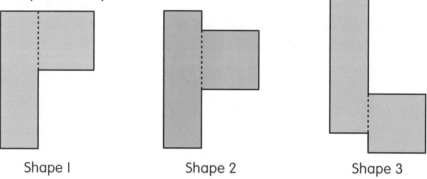

Shape I   Shape 2   Shape 3

a What can you say about the areas of these composite shapes? Work out the area of each shape.

b Without measuring, can you find the perimeter of each shape? Work out the perimeter where possible.

Let's Practise!

II Find the area and perimeter of this shape.

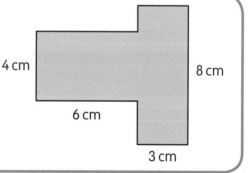

4 cm

6 cm

8 cm

3 cm

Let's Practise!

12 Two squares with 2 cm sides are cut out of a rectangle 10 cm by 5 cm. Find the area and perimeter of the remaining shape.

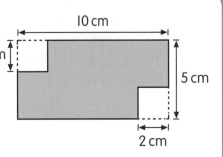

13 This shape is made up of two rectangles measuring 7 cm by 3 cm each and a square with 4 cm sides.
Find the area and perimeter of the shape.

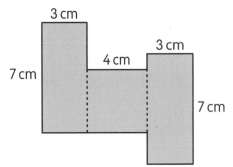

14 a Divide this trapezium into a rectangle and a triangle and find their areas. Then find the area of the trapezium.

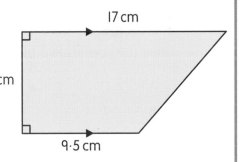

b By dividing the trapezium into two triangles, find its area.

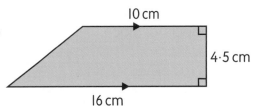

15 a Divide this shape into two right-angled triangles and find their areas. Then find the area of the shape.

b Find the perimeter of the shape.

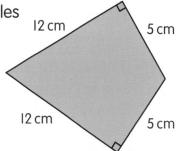

Let's Practise!

16 This diagram shows two triangles ACD and BCD in a square with 8 cm sides. Find the area of the shaded part.

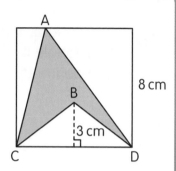

17 A running track is made up of two semicircles and two sides of a rectangle as shown. Find the length of the track.

$\left(\text{Take } \pi = \frac{22}{7}\right)$

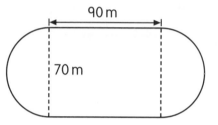

18 This diagram shows two quadrants of a circle in a rectangle. Taking $\pi = 3.14$, calculate the area and perimeter of the shaded part.

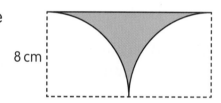

19 🔢 Find the area and perimeter of the shape shown. Give your answer to 1 decimal place.

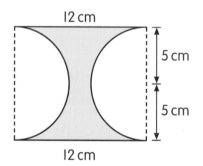

20 🔢 AB and CD are two perpendicular diameters. If AB = 54 cm, find the area of the shaded part. Give your answer to 1 decimal place. (Take $\pi = 3.14$)

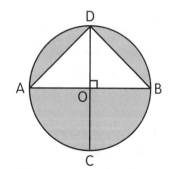

Let's Practise!

21 This diagram shows two quadrants in a square. Taking $\pi = \frac{22}{7}$, find the area and perimeter of the shaded part.

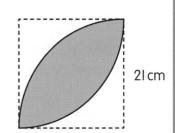

21 cm

22 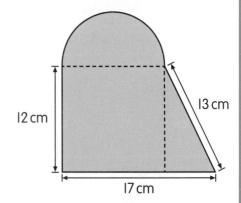 This shape is made up of a semicircle, a square and a triangle. Find the area and perimeter of the shape. Give your answers to 2 decimal places.

12 cm

13 cm

17 cm

23 This diagram shows a circle and 2 identical quadrants. The diameter of the circle is 14 cm. Find the area and perimeter of the shaded part.

$\left(\text{Take } \pi = \frac{22}{7}\right)$

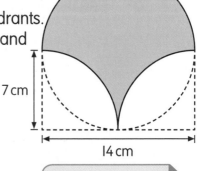

7 cm

14 cm

Practice Book 6B, p.91

Maths Journal

24 Write down the steps to find the area of the shaded part of this diagram. Use the following terms to help you:

semicircle   **quadrant**   **square**   **subtract**

Let's Wrap It Up!

You have learnt to:

- find the area and perimeter of shapes related to squares, rectangles, triangles, circles, semicircles and quadrants.

Let's Revise!

25 This shape is made up of a rectangle and a triangle.

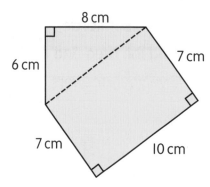

a Find the perimeter of the shape.

Perimeter of shape = 6 + 8 + 7 + 10 + 7
= 38 cm

b How can you find the area of this shape?
Work out the area of the shape.

Area of right-angled triangle = $\frac{1}{2} \times 6 \times 8$
= 24 cm²

Area of rectangle = 7 × 10
= 70 cm²

Area of shape = 24 + 70
= 94 cm²

Put On Your Thinking Caps!

26 ABCD is a rectangle 12 cm by 8 cm and BE = ED. Explain why triangles ABE and ADE are equal in area. Find the area of triangle ABE.

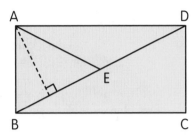

27 This shape is made up of two quadrants of a circle with a radius of 10 cm. The dotted lines enclose a rectangle 8 cm by 6 cm. Find the area and perimeter of the shape. (Take π = 3·14)

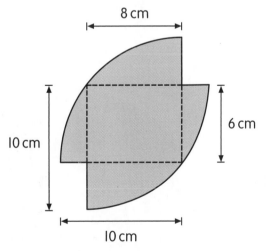

8 cm

6 cm

10 cm

10 cm

Practice Book 6B, p.98   Practice Book 6B, p.101

Unit 11

Volume of Solids and Liquids

Let's Learn!

 **Volume of solids**

 Let's revise volume.

1

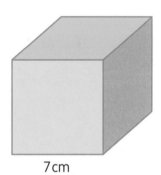

Volume of a cube
= Length × Width × Height

A cube has the same length, width and height.

7 cm

Volume of the cube = ☐ × ☐ × ☐

= ☐ cm³

2

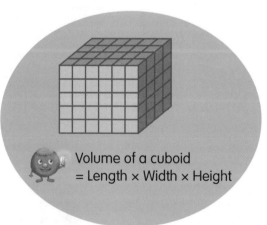

Volume of a cuboid
= Length × Width × Height

5 cm
4 cm
6 cm

Volume of the cuboid = ☐ × ☐ × ☐

= ☐ cm³

3 A cuboid has a volume of 72 cm³. Its length is 4 cm and its width is 3 cm. Find its height.

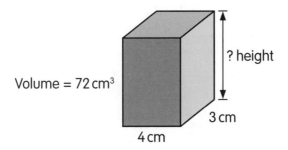

Volume = 72 cm³

? height

3 cm

4 cm

Method I

Volume of cuboid = length × width × height

4 × 3 × height = 72

12 × height = 72

So height = 72 ÷ 12

= 6 cm

The height of the cuboid is 6 cm.

3 × 2 = 6
So 2 = 6 ÷ 3

In the same way
12 × height = 72
So height = 72 ÷ 12

Method 2

4 × 3 × height = 72

So height = $\frac{72^{18}}{4 \times 3_{1}}$

= 6 cm

The height of the cuboid is 6 cm.

$\frac{72}{4 \times 3}$ is the same as 72 ÷ 12.

Home Maths Ask your child to measure the length, width and height of some cubical or cuboid objects and then to find the volume of each object.

4 The volume of a cuboid is 162 cm³. Its width is 6 cm and its height is 3 cm. Find the length of the cuboid.

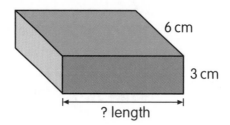

6 cm

3 cm

? length

Length × ◯ × ◯ = ◯

So length = $\dfrac{◯}{◯ \times ◯}$

= ◯ cm

The length of the cuboid is ◯ cm.

5 A cuboid tank has a base area of 600 cm². Find its height if its capacity is 5·4 ℓ.

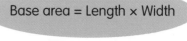

Base area = Length × Width

Capacity of tank = 5·4 ℓ = 5400 cm³

Capacity of tank = length × width × height

= base area × height

So height = capacity of tank ÷ base area

= 5400 ÷ 600

= 9 cm

The height of the tank is 9 cm.

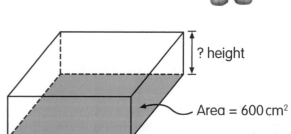

? height

Area = 600 cm²

6 The diagram below shows a cuboid with a volume of 117 cm³. The area of the square face is 9 cm². What is the length of the cuboid?

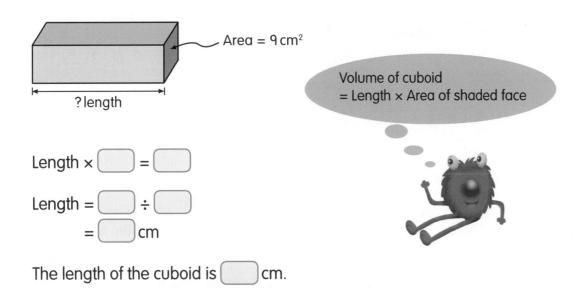

Area = 9 cm²

? length

Volume of cuboid
= Length × Area of shaded face

Length × ⬚ = ⬚

Length = ⬚ ÷ ⬚

= ⬚ cm

The length of the cuboid is ⬚ cm.

7 A cuboid block with a length of 16 cm and a height of 6 cm has a volume of 1448 cm³. Find its width to 1 decimal place.

Press	Display
C	0
1 4 4 8	1448
÷ (1 6 × 6)	(16 × 6)
=	15.08333333

16 × 6 × width = 1448

So width = $\dfrac{1448}{16 \times 6}$

= $\dfrac{1448}{96}$

≈ 15·1 cm.

The width of the cuboid block is 15·1 cm.

8 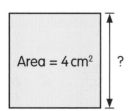 The volume of a cuboid is 1011 cm³. Its length is 12 cm and its width is 7 cm.

Find its height to 2 decimal places.

$\boxed{} \times \boxed{} \times$ height $= \boxed{}$

So height $= \dfrac{\boxed{}}{\boxed{} \times \boxed{}}$

$\approx \boxed{}$ cm

The height of the cuboid is $\boxed{}$ cm.

9 The area of a square is 4 cm². Find the length of one side of the square.

Area = 4 cm² ?

We write the **square root** of a number like this:
$\sqrt{4}, \sqrt{9}, \sqrt{16}, \ldots$

Side × Side = 4
4 = 2 × 2, so the length of one side of the square is 2 cm.

We say the **square root** of 4 is 2 and we write $\sqrt{4} = 2$.

10 **a** $9 = 3 \times \boxed{}$
$\sqrt{9} = \boxed{}$

b $25 = \boxed{} \times \boxed{}$
$\sqrt{25} = \boxed{}$

11 Find:

a $\sqrt{16}$ 　　　　**b** $\sqrt{49}$ 　　　　**c** $\sqrt{64}$

12  Find the square root of 225.

Press	Display
C	0
√ 2 2 5	225
=	15

$\sqrt{225} = \boxed{}$

13 Find:

a $\sqrt{169}$ **b** $\sqrt{484}$ **c** $\sqrt{961}$

14 The shaded face of this cuboid is a square. Its length is 10 cm and its volume is 360 cm³. Find the length of one side of the square face.

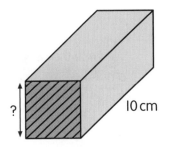

Volume of cuboid
= Area of square face × Length

Side × Side = 36 cm²
Side = $\sqrt{36}$

Area of square face × 10 = 360

Area of square face = $\frac{360}{10}$ = 36 cm²

Length of one side = $\sqrt{36}$
= 6 cm

15 A cuboid container with a height of 5 cm has a square base. Its capacity is 980 cm³. Find the length of one side of the square base.

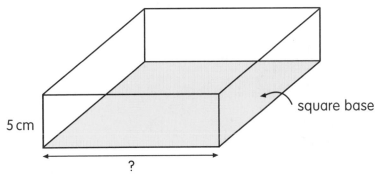

square base

5 cm

?

Area of square base × ☐ = ☐

Area of square face = $\frac{☐}{☐}$ = ☐ cm²

Length of one side = ☐
= ☐ cm

16 The volume of a cube is $8\,\text{cm}^3$. Find the length of one edge of the cube.

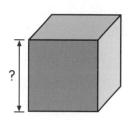

Volume = $8\,\text{cm}^3$

?

Edge × Edge × Edge = 8
$8 = 2 \times 2 \times 2$
So the length of one edge of the cube is 2 cm.

We say the **cube root** of 8 is 2 and we write $\sqrt[3]{8} = 2$.

We write the **cube root** of a number like this:
$\sqrt[3]{8}, \sqrt[3]{27}, \sqrt[3]{64}, \ldots$

17 **a** $27 = 3 \times 3 \times \boxed{}$

$\sqrt[3]{27} = \boxed{}$

b $64 = \boxed{} \times \boxed{} \times 4$

$\sqrt[3]{64} = \boxed{}$

18 Find:
a $\sqrt[3]{1}$

b $\sqrt[3]{125}$

19 Find the cube root of 729.

Press	Display
C	0
$\sqrt[3]{}$ 7 2 9	729
=	9

$\sqrt[3]{729} = \boxed{}$

20 Find:

a $\sqrt[3]{343}$

b $\sqrt[3]{512}$

c $\sqrt[3]{1728}$

21 The volume of a cube is 216 cm³. What is the length of each edge?

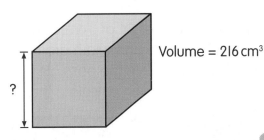

Volume = 216 cm³

Volume of cube = 216 cm³

Length of each edge = $\sqrt[3]{216}$

= 6 cm

Edge × Edge × Edge = 216

Edge = $\sqrt[3]{216}$

22 The volume of a cubical block of wood is 1331 cm³. Find the length of one edge of the block.

Volume of the block = 1331 cm³

Length of one edge = ⬚

= ⬚ cm

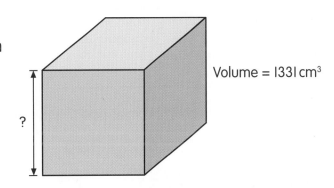

Volume = 1331 cm³

?

Activity

23 **a** The length, width and height of a cuboid are measured in whole centimetres. Its volume is 144 cm³ and its length is 6 cm. Copy the table below and fill in the possible values of the width and height of the cuboid.

Length (cm)	Width (cm)	Height (cm)	Volume (cm³)
6	⬚	⬚	144
6	⬚	⬚	144
6	⬚	⬚	144
6	⬚	⬚	144

Activity

b A cuboid container has a height of 5 cm. The perimeter of the base is 20 cm and its length and width are in whole centimetres. Copy the table below and fill in the possible values of the length and the width of the container. Then calculate the volume of the container.

Height (cm)	Length (cm)	Width (cm)	Volume (cm³)
5			
5			
5			
5			
5			

c Which container has the largest volume?

Let's Explore!

24 Work in pairs. Copy and complete the table.

Edge of Cube (cm)	Volume of Cube (cm³)
1	
2	
4	
8	

What can you conclude about the volume of a cube when the length of each edge is doubled? State your conclusion like this:

When the length of each edge of a cube is doubled, the volume is ⬜ times that of the original cube.

Let's Explore!

25 A cube has a volume of 27 cm³. What is the increase in volume if the length of each edge is doubled?

Maths Journal

26 Complete these statements.

a 17 × 17 = 289, so 17 is the ☐ of ☐.

b 15 × 15 × 15 = 3375, so 15 is the ☐ of ☐.

27 Peter does not understand why the volume of the cuboid tank is equal to *Area of base × Height*. How would you explain this to Peter?

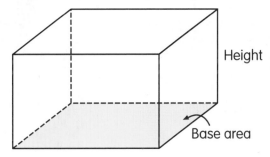

Height

Base area

Let's Practise!

28 🖩 For each cuboid, find the length of the unknown edge.

a

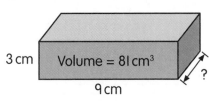

3 cm
Volume = 81 cm³
9 cm
?

b

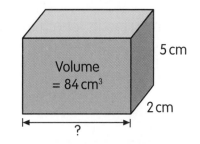

5 cm
Volume = 84 cm³
2 cm
?

Let's Practise!

29 For each cube, find the length of the unknown edge.

a

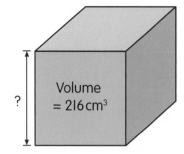

? Volume = 216 cm³

b

? Volume = 2197 cm³

30 For each cuboid, find the length of one side of the square face.

a

3 cm   Volume = 768 cm³

b

13 cm

Volume = 1573 cm³

31 The width of a cuboid container is 4 cm and its height is 17 cm. The capacity of the container is 1226 cm³. Find its length to the nearest cm.

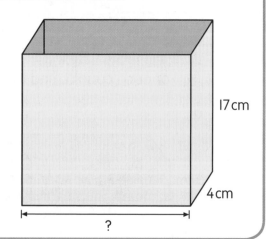

17 cm

4 cm

?

Let's Practise!

32 Find the volume of Cuboid A below. If Cuboid B has the same volume as Cuboid A, find the height of Cuboid B.

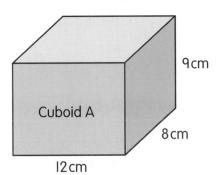

Cuboid A — 9 cm, 8 cm, 12 cm

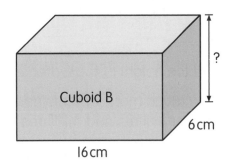

Cuboid B — ?, 6 cm, 16 cm

33 What is the volume of Cube X? If Cube Y has a volume equal to $\frac{1}{8}$ of the volume of Cube X, find the length of its edge.

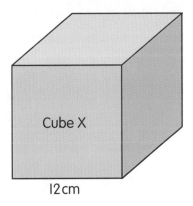

Cube X — 12 cm

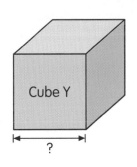

Cube Y — ?

34 A cuboid block 16 cm long has two square faces. A cube of volume 343 cm³ is cut from the cuboid block as shown. Find the volume of the remaining block.

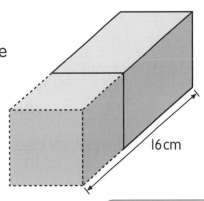

16 cm

Practice Book 6B, p.103

Let's Learn!

Volume of liquids

1 A cuboid tank measuring 24 cm by 20 cm by 14 cm contains 3·84 ℓ of water.

a Find the height of the water level.

b How much more water is needed to fill the tank completely? Give your answer in litres and millilitres. (1 ℓ = 1000 ml)

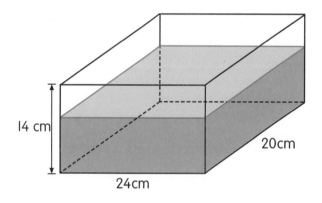

14 cm

20cm

24cm

We can measure the volume of water in cubic centimetres (cm³) or millilitres (ml).

1 cm³ = 1 ml

a Volume of water = 3·84 × 1000
= 3840 cm³

Height of water level = $\dfrac{3840}{24 \times 20}$

= 8 cm

b Capacity of tank = 24 × 20 × 14
= 6720 cm³
= 6720 ml

Amount of water needed = 6720 − 3840
= 2880 ml
= 2 ℓ 880 ml

2 An empty cuboid container has a square base with 10 cm sides and a height of 30 cm. It is filled with 1·2 ℓ of water.

  a Find the height of the water level.

  b How many more litres of water are needed to fill the tank completely?
  (1 ℓ = 1000 ml)

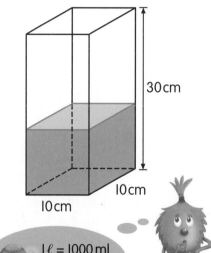

  a Volume of water = ⬚ cm³

  Height of water level = ⬚

  = ⬚ cm

  b Capacity of tank = ⬚ × ⬚ × ⬚

  = ⬚ ml

  Amount of water needed = ⬚ − ⬚

  = ⬚ ml

  = ⬚ ℓ

1 ℓ = 1000 ml
= 1000 cm³

3 A cuboid tank 30 cm by 12 cm by 20 cm is $\frac{1}{2}$ full of water. Find the volume of water in the tank. How much more water is needed to make the tank $\frac{3}{4}$ full?

Give your answer in litres. (1 ℓ = 1000 cm³)

Height of water level = $\frac{1}{2}$ × 20

= 10 cm

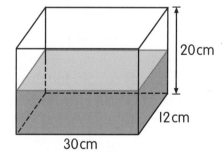

Volume of water = 30 × 12 × 10
= 3600 cm³
= 3·6 ℓ

Height of water level when tank is $\frac{3}{4}$ full = $\frac{3}{4}$ × 20

= 15 cm

Increase in height of water level = 15 − 10
= 5 cm

Volume of water needed = 30 × 12 × 5
= 1800 cm³
= 1·8 ℓ

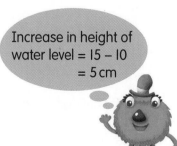

4 The base of an empty cuboid tank measures 50 cm by 40 cm. It is filled with water up to $\frac{1}{3}$ of its height. If the volume of water in the tank is 96 ℓ, find the height of the tank. (I ℓ = 1000 cm³)

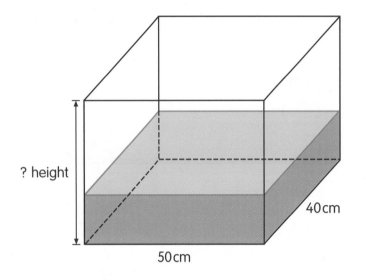

? height

50 cm

40 cm

Convert the volume of water from litres (ℓ) to cubic centimetres (cm³).

Volume of water = ☐ cm³

Height of water level = ☐

= ☐ cm

Height of tank = ☐ × ☐

= ☐ cm

5 An empty cuboid tank measures 30 cm by 20 cm by 35 cm. Water flows into the tank at 7 ℓ per minute. How many minutes will it take to fill the whole tank with water? (I ℓ = 1000 cm³)

Capacity of tank = 30 × 20 × 35
= 21 000 cm³
= 21 ℓ

7 ℓ ⟶ I min
21 ℓ ⟶ 21 ÷ 7
= 3 mins

Time taken = 3 mins

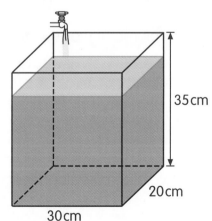

35 cm

20 cm

30 cm

6 A cuboid tank measuring 80 cm by 50 cm by 45 cm is filled with water flowing from a tap at 9 litres per minute. After how long will the tank be $\frac{3}{4}$ full? (1 ℓ = 1000 cm³)

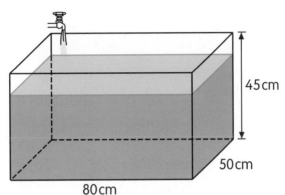

45 cm

50 cm

80 cm

Volume of water in tank = ⬜ × ⬜ × ⬜ × ⬜

= ⬜ cm³

= ⬜ ℓ

9 ℓ ⟶ 1 min

⬜ ℓ ⟶ ⬜ ÷ ⬜

= ⬜ mins

Time taken = ⬜ mins

7 🖩 A cuboid tank has a square base and a height of 35 cm. It is filled with water and the volume of water in the tank is 7·875 ℓ. Find the length of one edge of the base. (1 ℓ = 1000 cm³)

Volume of water = Area of base × Height

Area of base × 35 = 7·875 × 1000

= 7875

Area of base = 7875 ÷ 35

= 225 cm²

Edge of base = $\sqrt{225}$

= 15 cm

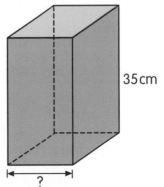

35 cm

?

8 A cuboid tin with a length of 28 cm has two square faces. When full, it can hold 9·072 ℓ of water. Find the length of one side of each square face. (1 ℓ = 1000 cm³)

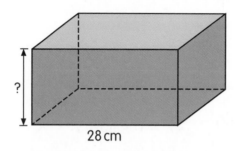

28 cm

Volume of water = Area of square face × 28

Area of square face × ⬭ = ⬭ × ⬭

= ⬭

Area of square face = ⬭ ÷ ⬭

= ⬭ cm²

Length of one side = ⬭

= ⬭ cm

9 A cubical container is completely filled with 2·197 ℓ of water. Find the area of the base of the container. (1 ℓ = 1000 cm³)

Capacity of cubical container = Volume of water
= 2·197 × 1000
= 2197 cm³

Length of one edge = $\sqrt[3]{2197}$
= 13 cm

Area of base = 13 × 13
= 169 cm²

?

10 A cubical tank is $\frac{2}{3}$ full of water. The volume of water in the tank is $18\,\ell$.
Find the area of the base of the tank. ($1\,\ell = 1000\,cm^3$)

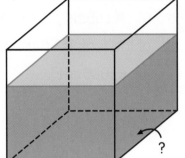

$\frac{2}{3}$ of capacity of tank $\longrightarrow$ $18\,\ell$

$\frac{1}{3}$ of capacity of tank $\longrightarrow$ $18\,\ell \div 2$

$\qquad\qquad\qquad\qquad = 9\,\ell$

Capacity of tank $\longrightarrow$ 3×9

$\qquad\qquad\qquad = 27\,\ell$

Capacity of tank = ☐ ℓ

$\qquad\qquad\quad = $ ☐ cm^3

Length of one edge = ☐

$\qquad\qquad\qquad = $ ☐ cm

Area of base = ☐ $\times$ ☐

$\qquad\qquad = $ ☐ cm^2

Activity

11 Work in pairs. You want to make an open cuboid container with a capacity of $1\,\ell$ with a base area of $100\,cm^2$. The length and width of your container are in whole centimetres. Copy the table below and fill in some possible measurements of your container.

Capacity (ℓ)	Base Area (cm²)	Height (cm)	Length (cm)	Width (cm)
1	100	☐	☐	☐
1	100	☐	☐	☐
1	100	☐	☐	☐
1	100	☐	☐	☐
1	100	☐	☐	☐

Let's Practise!

12 A cuboid tank can hold 1·8 ℓ of water when it is full. The length of the tank is 30 cm and its width is 8 cm. Find the height of the tank. (1 ℓ = 1000 cm³)

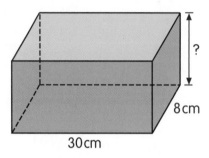

13 A cubical tank with an edge of 12 cm is half filled with water. Find the volume of water in the tank in millilitres. (1 ml = 1 cm³)

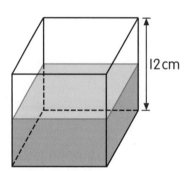

Let's Practise!

14 🖩 A cuboid tank has a length of 12 cm, width of 8 cm and height of 37·5 cm. 2·4 ℓ of water is poured into the tank.

   a What is the height of the water level in centimetres?

   b How many more litres of water must be poured into the tank to fill it to the brim? (1 ℓ = 1000 cm³)

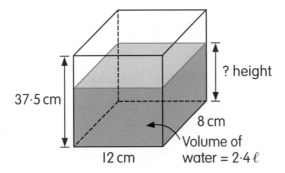

37·5 cm

? height

8 cm

12 cm

Volume of water = 2·4 ℓ

15 A cuboid tank that has a base area of 300 cm² and a height of 15 cm is full of water. After 1·75 ℓ of water is poured out, how much water is left in the tank? Give your answer in litres. (1 ℓ = 1000 cm³)

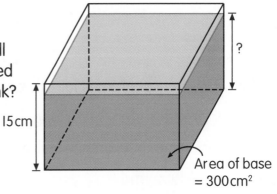

?

15 cm

Area of base = 300 cm²

16 🖩 A cuboid tank measuring 25 cm by 16 cm by 20 cm is $\frac{1}{2}$ full of water.

   a Find the volume of water. Give your answer in litres.

   b If 1·5 ℓ of water is poured out of the tank, what is the height of the new water level? (1 ℓ = 1000 cm³)

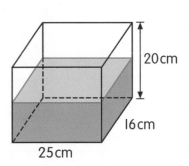

20 cm

16 cm

25 cm

Let's Practise!

17 A cubical tank is $\frac{3}{4}$ full of water. The volume of water in the tank is 6 ℓ. Find the length of each edge of the tank. (1 ℓ = 1000 cm³)

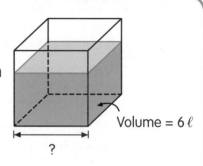

Volume = 6 ℓ

?

18 A cuboid tank with a square base with an area of 625 cm² is $\frac{2}{3}$ full of water.

    a Find the length of one side of the base.

    b If the volume of water in the tank is 15 ℓ, find the height of the tank.
    (1 ℓ = 1000 cm³)

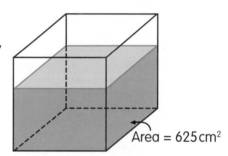

Area = 625 cm²

19 A cylindrical drum is full of water. When the water is poured into a cuboid tank measuring 30 cm long, 25 cm wide and 24 cm high, it fills up $\frac{3}{4}$ of the tank. Find the capacity of the drum. Give your answer in litres.
(1 ℓ = 1000 cm³)

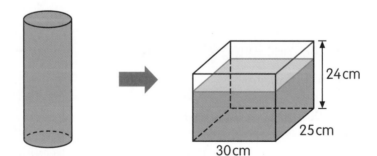

24 cm

25 cm

30 cm

Let's Practise!

20 An empty cuboid tank has a base area of 3000 cm² and a height of 32 cm. It is filled with water flowing from a tap at 12 ℓ per minute. How many minutes will it take to fill half of the tank with water? (1 ℓ = 1000 cm³)

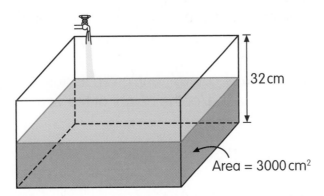

32 cm

Area = 3000 cm²

21 A cubical tank of edge 60 cm is $\frac{3}{4}$ full of water. A tap drains water out of the tank at 9 ℓ per minute. How long will it take to drain half of the volume of water out of the tank? (1 ℓ = 1000 cm³)

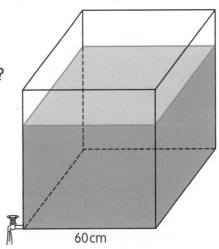

60 cm

Practice Book 6B, p.117

Let's Wrap It Up!

You have learnt to:

- find one edge of a cubical or cuboid tank given its volume and:
  - **i** two other edges, or
  - **ii** area of one of the faces/base
- use a calculator to find the square root and cube root of a number
- find one side of the square base of a cubical or cuboid tank given its volume and the height
- find one edge of a cube or cubical tank given its volume
- find the volume of water and/or the height of the water level in a cubical or cuboid container.

Let's Revise!

22 A cubical tank with an edge of 15 cm is $\frac{1}{3}$ filled with water. The water is then poured into an empty cuboid tank with a length of 15 cm and a width of 10 cm. Find the height of the water level in the cuboid tank.

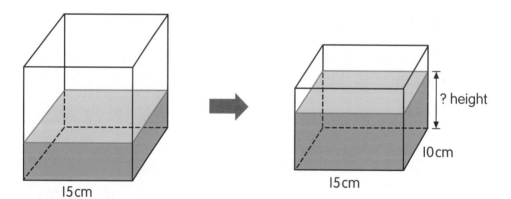

Volume of water in cubical tank $= \frac{1}{3} \times (15 \times 15 \times 15)$

$\qquad\qquad\qquad\qquad\qquad\qquad\quad = 1125\,\text{cm}^3$

Height of water in cuboid tank $= 1125 \div (15 \times 10)$

$\qquad\qquad\qquad\qquad\qquad\qquad\quad = 7\cdot5\,\text{cm}$

Let's Wrap It Up!

23 A cubical container with an edge of 36 cm is $\frac{2}{3}$ full of water. When the water is poured into an empty cuboid tank with a square base with an area of 576 cm², it fills up $\frac{3}{4}$ of the tank.

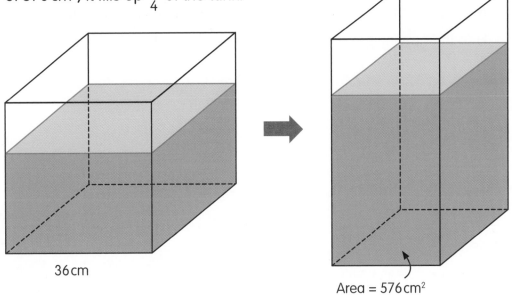

36 cm

Area = 576 cm²

Find:

a the length of one side of the square base of the cuboid tank

Length of one side of the square base = $\sqrt{576}$
                                      = 24 cm

b the height of the water level of the tank, and

Volume of water = $\frac{2}{3}$ × 36 × 36 × 36
                = 31 104 cm³

Height of water level = 31 104 ÷ 576
                      = 54 cm

c the height of the tank.

$\frac{3}{4}$ of the height = 54 cm

Height of the tank = $\frac{4}{3}$ × 54
                   = 72 cm

Put On Your Thinking Caps!

24 A drum contains 9 ℓ more water than a cuboid tank with a base of 25 cm by 20 cm. When 3 ℓ of water is poured from the tank into the drum, the volume of water in the drum is II times the volume of water in the tank. Find the new height of the water level in the tank. (I ℓ = 1000 cm³)

Practice Book 6B, p.129 ▷   Practice Book 6B, p.131 ▷

Think It Through

Whole numbers

1 Tim's age now is a multiple of 5. In one year's time, his age will be a multiple of 7 and in two years' time, it will be a multiple of 11. If he is less than 60 years old, how old is Tim now?

Solve the problem step by step.

Step	Tim's Possible Age
a List the multiples of 5 which are less than 60.	5, 10, 15, 20, 25, 30, 35, 40, 45, 50, 55
b To find his age in one year's time, add 1 to each multiple of 5.	6, 11, 16, 21, 26, 31, 36, 41, 46, 51, 56
c Pick out the multiples of 7.	21, 56
d To find his age in two years' time, add 1 to each multiple of 7.	22, 57
e Pick out the multiple of 11.	22

In two years' time, Tim will be 22 years old.

Tim is 20 years old now.

2 James has counted 16 spiders and birds in his garden. He asks his friend, Ruby, to guess the number of spiders and birds he has counted by telling her that there are 92 legs altogether. How many spiders and birds are there?

Make a list.

Number of Birds	Number of Legs	Number of Spiders	Number of Legs	Total Number of Legs
8	8 × 2 = 16	8	8 × 8 = 64	16 + 64 = 80
7	14	9	72	86
6	12	10	80	92 ✓

James counted 6 birds and 10 spiders.

Let's Practise!

3   Sita's age is a factor of 30. Next year her age will be a factor of 32. In two years' time her age will be a factor of 40. How old is Sita now?

4   In a football tournament, there are 6 teams. Each team plays against each of the other teams twice. How many matches are played altogether?

5   8 members of a committee attend a meeting. If every member shakes hands with each of the other members, how many handshakes are there altogether?

6   A bag of marbles is to be shared among some children. If each child gets 4 marbles, 3 marbles are left over. If each child gets 5 marbles, 2 more marbles are needed.

    a   How many children are there?

    b   How many marbles are there?

7   In a toy shop there are 24 pedal cars and tricycles altogether. Each pedal car has 4 wheels. The pedal cars and tricycles have a total of 81 wheels.

    a   How many tricycles are there?

    b   How many pedal cars are there?

8   A metal bucket full of sand has a total mass of 10 kg. When it is full of water, its mass is 4 kg. If the mass of the sand is 3 times that of the water, find the mass of the bucket.

Fractions

9 $\frac{1}{4}$ of the spectators at a football match were children. The number of women was $\frac{1}{3}$ of the number of men. If there were 1680 spectators, how many men were there?

$1 - \frac{1}{4} = \frac{3}{4}$

$\frac{3}{4}$ of the spectators were men and women.

> Find the number of men and women who were at the match.

Number of men and women $= \frac{3}{4}$ of the spectators

$\qquad\qquad\qquad\qquad\quad = \frac{3}{4} \times 1680$

$\qquad\qquad\qquad\qquad\quad = 1260$

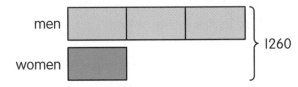

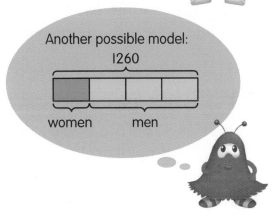

Another possible model:

The model above shows that:
4 units ⟶ 1260
1 unit ⟶ 1260 ÷ 4 = 315
3 units ⟶ 3 × 315 = 945

There were 945 men.

10 At a concert, $\frac{2}{3}$ of the number of women were equal to $\frac{4}{5}$ of the number of men. If there were 1540 people at the concert, how many men were there?

The model above shows that:
11 units ⟶ 1540
1 unit ⟶ 1540 ÷ 11 = 140
5 units ⟶ 5 × 140 = 700

There were 700 men.

Let's Practise!

11. On a Sunday, $\frac{1}{3}$ of the visitors to the wildlife park were children. The number of men was $\frac{3}{5}$ of the number of women. If there were 1860 visitors, how many of them were women?

12. John's age is $\frac{1}{4}$ of his father's age. His father is 48 years old. In how many years' time will John's age be $\frac{1}{3}$ of his father's age?

13. Miss Taylor went shopping. She bought a pair of trainers for £30 and spent $\frac{2}{3}$ of the remainder on a watch. She was then left with $\frac{1}{5}$ of the money she had at first. How much money did Miss Taylor have at first?

14. $\frac{3}{4}$ of the number of girls in a school is equal to $\frac{1}{2}$ of the number of boys. If the school has 1420 pupils, how many of them are boys?

15. $\frac{2}{5}$ of a packet of 40 nuts were peanuts. After some peanuts were eaten, the fraction of peanuts in the packet became $\frac{1}{3}$. How many peanuts were eaten?

Decimals

 16 The total mass of 4 packs of mushrooms and 2 bags of potatoes is 4·5 kg. A bag of potatoes is 3 times as heavy as a pack of mushrooms. Find the total mass of a bag of potatoes and a pack of mushrooms.

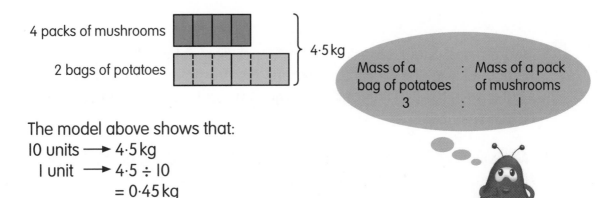

4 packs of mushrooms

2 bags of potatoes

4·5 kg

Mass of a bag of potatoes : Mass of a pack of mushrooms
3 : 1

The model above shows that:
10 units ⟶ 4·5 kg
1 unit ⟶ 4·5 ÷ 10
= 0·45 kg

The mass of a pack of mushrooms is 0·45 kg.

0·45 × 3 = 1·35

The mass of a bag of potatoes is 1·35 kg.

0·45 + 1·35 = 1·8

The total mass of a bag of potatoes and a pack of mushrooms is 1·8 kg.

Let's Practise!

17 3 jugs and 2 glasses can hold a total of 5·6 ℓ of water. The capacity of a jug is equal to the capacity of 6 glasses. Find the difference between the capacity of a jug and that of a glass.

18 A drum and a tank contain 16·8 ℓ of water altogether. When 2·4 ℓ of water is poured from the tank into the drum, the drum has 5 times as much water as that left in the tank. How much water was in the tank at first?

19 Millie thinks of a number. When she adds 22·5 to it, she gets 11 times the number. What is the number that Millie is thinking of?

20 Rover is 5·6 kg heavier than Rocky. Rocky is 3·8 kg heavier than Duke. If their total mass is 124·2 kg, find the mass of each dog.

21 A drum contains 11·6 ℓ more water than a tank. When 3·2 ℓ of water are poured from the tank into the drum, the drum has 11 times as much water as that left in the tank. How much water is left in the tank?

Ratio

 22 David's sticker collection contained football and wildlife stickers. $\frac{2}{3}$ of the total number of stickers were wildlife stickers. The wildlife stickers were either animal or plant stickers. The ratio of the number of animal stickers to the number of plant stickers was 5:3.

If there were 21 plant stickers, how many football stickers were there?

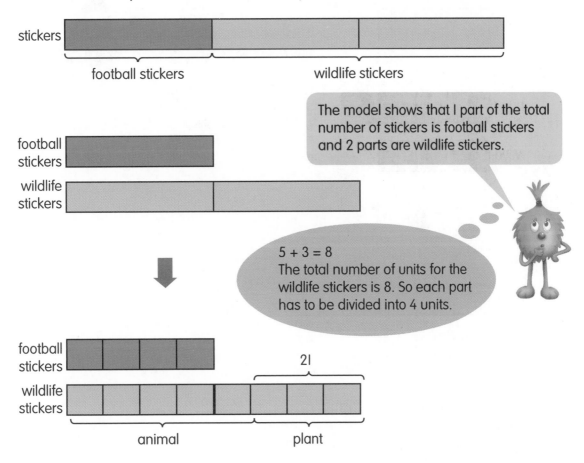

stickers

football stickers   wildlife stickers

football stickers

wildlife stickers

The model shows that 1 part of the total number of stickers is football stickers and 2 parts are wildlife stickers.

$5 + 3 = 8$
The total number of units for the wildlife stickers is 8. So each part has to be divided into 4 units.

football stickers

wildlife stickers

21

animal   plant

3 units → 21 stickers
1 unit → 21 ÷ 3
     = 7 stickers
4 units → 4 × 7
     = 28 football stickers

football stickers → 4 units
animal stickers → 5 units
plant stickers → 3 units

There were 28 football stickers in David's sticker collection.

23 The ratio of the number of sweets Ruby had to the number of sweets Miya had was 4:3 at first. After Miya gave half of her sweets to Ruby, Ruby had 128 sweets more than Miya. How many sweets did Ruby have in the end?

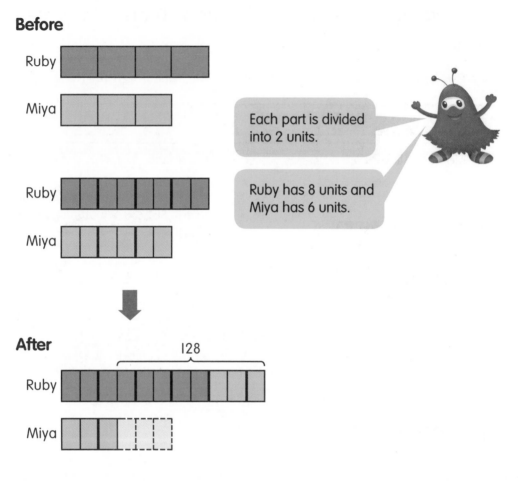

Before

Ruby

Miya

Each part is divided into 2 units.

Ruby has 8 units and Miya has 6 units.

Ruby

Miya

After

128

Ruby

Miya

The model above shows that:

8 units ⟶ 128 sweets

1 unit ⟶ 128 ÷ 8

= 16 sweets

11 units ⟶ 11 × 16

= 176 sweets

Ruby had 176 sweets in the end.

24 In a box the number of 10p coins and 20p coins were in the ratio 2 : 1. Some 10p coins were taken out and replaced by a number of 20p coins of the same value, so that the total sum of money in the box remained the same. Then the ratio of the number of 10p coins to the number of 20p coins became 1 : 2. If the amount of the money in the box is less than £4, find:

a the amount of money in the box

b the number of 10p coins which were taken out and replaced with 20p coins.

a

Make a table of the equivalent ratios of the number of 10p coins and 20p coins before and after the coins are replaced.

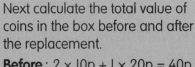
Next calculate the total value of coins in the box before and after the replacement.

Before : 2 × 10p + 1 × 20p = 40p
After : 1 × 10p + 2 × 20p = 50p

Before Replacement		After Replacement	
Number of Coins		Number of Coins	
10p : 20p	Total Value (p)	10p : 20p	Total Value (p)
2 : 1	40	1 : 2	50
4 : 2	80	2 : 4	100
6 : 3	120	3 : 6	150
8 : 4	160	**4 : 8**	**200**
10 : 5	**200**	5 : 10	250

From the table, the total sum of money in the box was 200p or £2.

The total value of coins remained the same before and after the replacement of the 10p coins with 20p coins.

b 10 − 4 = 6

Six 10p coins were taken out and replaced with 20p coins.

Let's Practise!

25 The ratio of the number of watermelons to the number of pineapples in a supermarket was $1:3$. If $\frac{2}{9}$ of the pineapples were sold, only 35 pineapples would be left. How many watermelons were there in the supermarket?

26 The ratio of the amount of money Mr Thompson had to the amount of money Mr Ali had was $1:2$ at first. After Mr Ali gave $\frac{1}{3}$ of his money to Mr Thompson, Mr Ali had £42 less than Mr Thompson. How much money did each person have in the end?

27 The ratio of the number of Japanese cars to the number of German cars in a showroom is $3:4$. The German cars are either red or black. The number of red cars is $\frac{2}{3}$ of the number of black cars. If there are 52 more black cars than red cars:

a how many cars are there altogether in the showroom?

b how many cars are Japanese cars?

28 Mr Holden had muffins and sandwiches in the ratio $5:2$ at first. He sold 18 muffins and made 15 more sandwiches. In the end, he found that he had as many muffins as sandwiches.

a How many muffins did he have at first?

b How many sandwiches did he have in the end?

Let's Practise!

29 The ratio of the number of fish in Tank A to the number of fish in Tank B was 8 : 19. When Jake transferred 4 fish from Tank B to Tank A, there were 36 fewer fish in Tank A than Tank B. How many fish were there in each tank at first?

30 Mr Green, Mr Lee and Miss Brook each had some money. The ratio of the amount of money Mr Green had to the amount of money Mr Lee had was 7 : 3 at first. Mr Green gave £48 to Miss Brook and Mr Lee borrowed £172 from Miss Brook. In the end, Mr Green had the same amount of money as Mr Lee.

a How much money did Mr Lee have at first?

b How much money did Mr Green and Mr Lee each have in the end?

31 Hardeep had some 20p coins and 50p coins in the ratio 3 : 2. He spent some 20p coins but his sister gave him some 50p coins with a total value that was equal to the amount of money he had spent. Then the ratio of the number of 20p coins to the number of 50p coins became 5 : 6.
If Hardeep had less than £15, find:

a the total amount of money he had

b the number of 20p coins he had spent.

Percentage

32 ▦ Farha bought 3 identical pieces of ribbon, Ribbon A, Ribbon B and Ribbon C. She cut off 90% of Ribbon A to wrap a present. Then she cut off 40% of Ribbon B to make a flower. Ribbon C was not used.
If the total length of ribbon left was 6·8 m:

a what was the original length of each piece of ribbon?

b what was the total length of ribbon she used?

a **Method I**

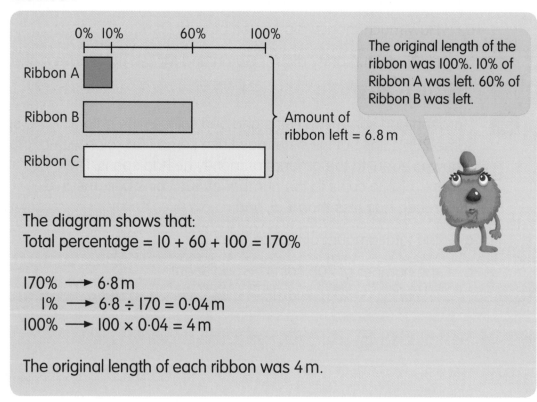

The diagram shows that:
Total percentage = 10 + 60 + 100 = 170%

170% ⟶ 6·8 m
1% ⟶ 6·8 ÷ 170 = 0·04 m
100% ⟶ 100 × 0·04 = 4 m

The original length of each ribbon was 4 m.

Method 2

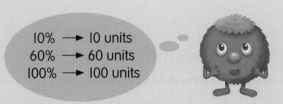

10% → 10 units
60% → 60 units
100% → 100 units

In its simplest form, the ratio of the number of units is 1 : 6 : 10.

Ribbon A

Ribbon B

Ribbon C

Amount of
ribbon left = 6.8 m

Total number of units = 1 + 6 + 10 = 17

17 units → 6.8 m
1 unit → 6.8 ÷ 17 = 0.4 m
10 units → 10 × 0.4 = 4 m

The original length of each ribbon was 4 m.

b   Total length of the 3 ribbons = 3 × 4
                                    = 12 m

12 m − 6.8 m = 5.2 m

She used 5.2 m of ribbon.

Let's Practise!

33 There were 35 pupils in the school Environment Club. 20% of them were boys. After 5 more pupils joined the club, the number of boys in the club increased to 25%. How many boys joined the club?

34 Mr Jessop had a total of 240 white loaves and brown loaves in his bakery. 60% of the loaves were white. After he sold a total of 80 white loaves and brown loaves, 55% of the loaves left were white. How many white loaves did he sell?

35 Mr Young planted apple, pear and cherry trees in his orchard. 25% of the trees were pear trees. There were 4 times as many apple trees as cherry trees. If there were 180 more apple trees than cherry trees, how many pear trees were there?

Speed

36 Mr Rahman and Mr Turnbull left York and drove a distance of 140 km to reach Liverpool. Mr Rahman started his journey at 13:50 and drove at an average speed of 56 km/h. Mr Turnbull started his journey half an hour later and drove along the same road. Both of them arrived in Liverpool at the same time. What was Mr Turnbull's average speed?

Draw a diagram to show the distance, time and speed.

Mr Rahman ⟶ 56 km/h

140 km

York   Liverpool

Mr Turnbull ⟶ ? km/h

First find the time taken by Mr Rahman.

Time taken by Mr Rahman = $\dfrac{140}{56}$

$= 2\dfrac{1}{2}$ h

Time = $\dfrac{\text{Distance}}{\text{Speed}}$

Time taken by Mr Turnbull = $2\dfrac{1}{2} - \dfrac{1}{2}$

$= 2$ h

Next find Mr Turnbull's average speed.

Speed = $\dfrac{\text{Distance}}{\text{Time}}$

Speed = $\dfrac{140}{2}$ h

$= 70$ km/h

Mr Turnbull's average speed was 70 km/h.

37 Marek drove from Sunnytown to Cloudside and then to Smartville. He began his journey at 10:00 a.m. He drove at an average speed of 48 km/h from Sunnytown to Cloudside which were 84 km apart. He stopped at Cloudside for 15 minutes and then continued his journey from Cloudside to Smartville which were 96 km apart. He drove at an average speed of 64 km/h from Cloudside to Smartville. What time did Marek arrive in Smartville?

First find the total time taken.

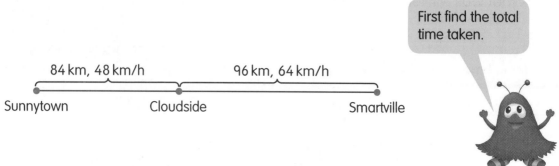

From Sunnytown to Cloudside:

Time = $\frac{84}{48}$

Time = $\frac{\text{Distance}}{\text{Speed}}$

= $1\frac{3}{4}$ h

= 1 h 45 mins

From Cloudside to Smartville:

Time = $\frac{96}{64}$

= $1\frac{1}{2}$ h

= 1 h 30 mins

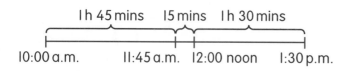

Marek arrived in Smartville at 1:30 p.m.

38 Mr Thomas cycled a distance of 28 km at an average speed of 12 km/h for the first part of his journey. He completed the rest of the journey in 45 minutes. If he arrived at his destination at 20:40, what time did he start his journey?

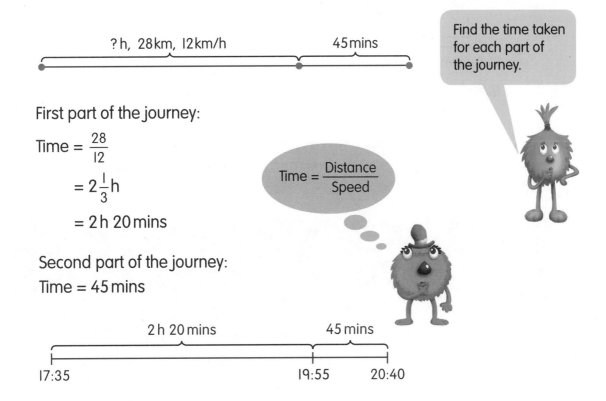

Find the time taken for each part of the journey.

First part of the journey:

$$\text{Time} = \frac{28}{12}$$

$$= 2\frac{1}{3}\text{ h}$$

$$= 2\text{ h } 20\text{ mins}$$

Time = $\dfrac{\text{Distance}}{\text{Speed}}$

Second part of the journey:
Time = 45 mins

Mr Thomas started his journey at 17:35.

39 Susan drove from Circletown to Squareville at a speed of 50 km/h. Joseph drove from Squareville to Circletown along the same road at a speed of 70 km/h. Both of them started their journey at 11:00 a.m. If the distance between Circletown and Squareville was 360 km, what time would they pass each other?

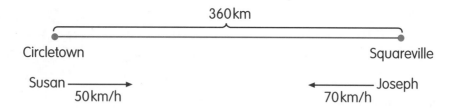

In each hour, Susan travelled 50 km whereas Joseph travelled 70 km. The table below shows the time taken and distance travelled by Susan and Joseph at each given period of time.

Time Taken	Distance Travelled by Susan	Distance Travelled by Joseph	Total Distance Travelled
1 h	50 km	70 km	120 km
2 h	100 km	140 km	240 km
3 h	150 km	210 km	360 km

From the table, after 3 hours, the total distance travelled by Susan and Joseph was 360 km. As this is the distance between Circletown and Squareville, this meant that they would pass each other 3 hours after 11:00 a.m.

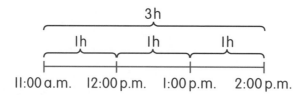

So they would pass each other at 2:00 p.m.

40 At 7:00 a.m., Mr Smith and Mr Williams left Robinstown for Bakerstown along the same road. When Mr Williams arrived at Bakerstown at 9:00 a.m., Mr Smith had just completed $\frac{3}{4}$ of the whole journey. Mr Smith travelled at an average speed of 20 km/h less than Mr Williams.

a Find the distance between the two towns.

b Find the average speed of Mr Williams.

a Time taken by Mr Williams to travel from Robinstown to Bakerstown = 2 h
Mr Williams' speed is 20 km/h faster than Mr Smith's speed. So for every 1 hour, Mr Williams is 20 km ahead of Mr Smith.

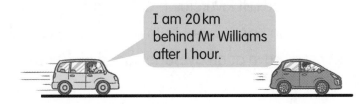

I am 20 km behind Mr Williams after 1 hour.

The table shows the difference in distance travelled by each person at 1 h intervals after leaving Robinstown.

Time After Leaving Robinstown	Distance that Mr Williams was Ahead of Mr Smith
1 h	20 km
2 h	40 km

After 2 h, Mr Williams arrived at Bakerstown and Mr Smith was 40 km behind Mr Williams.

1 unit ⟶ 40 km
4 units ⟶ 4 × 40
= 160 km

The distance between the two towns is 160 km.

b 2 h ⟶ 160 km
1 h ⟶ 160 ÷ 2
= 80 km

Mr Williams' speed was 80 km/h.

Let's Practise!

41 The cycling track at a stadium was 400 m. Hardeep and Millie cycled round the track once. Hardeep cycled at an average speed of 8 m/s. Millie started cycling 5 s later and both of them arrived at the end point at the same time.

    a Find the time Millie took to cycle 400 m.

    b Find Millie's average cycling speed. Give your answer to 1 decimal place.

42 Konrad and Mark each drove 210 km from Riverstown to Hillstown along the same road. Konrad left Riverstown at 8:05 p.m. and Mark left Riverstown half an hour later than Konrad, but both of them arrived in Hillstown at the same time. Konrad drove at an average speed of 60 km/h. Find Mark's average speed.

43 Miss Morris began cycling from her home to the beach at 7:48 a.m. She cycled at an average speed of 12 km/h. She arrived at the beach at 8:28 a.m. She was at the beach for $2\frac{1}{2}$ h and then cycled back to her home.

    a Find the distance between her home and the beach.

    b What time did she leave the beach?

44 Mr Lake drove for 2 hours at a speed of 72 km/h from Jamestown to Waterville. From Waterville to Hollystown, he drove for 3 hours at an average speed of 88 km/h. Find the total distance Mr Lake travelled from Jamestown to Hollystown.

45 Michael left Peterstown for Simonstown at 7:00 a.m. By 8:00 a.m., he had travelled 60 km, and he drove at this speed for the whole route. At 8:00 a.m., Maria left Peterstown and travelled at an average speed of 80 km/h along the same route. Both of them arrived at Simonstown at the same time. Find the distance between Peterstown and Simonstown.

46 Theo left Marshalltown at 09:00 and drove 220 km to Rosetown. He drove at an average speed of 70 km/h. An hour later, Jessica left Rosetown for Marshalltown, driving along the same road, at 80 km/h. At what distance from Marshalltown would they meet?